the
social media
marketing
book

Dan Zarrella

O'REILLY®

Beijing · Cambridge · Farnham · Köln · Sebastopol · Taipei · Tokyo

The Social Media Marketing Book

by Dan Zarrella

Copyright © 2010 Dan Zarrella. Printed in Canada.

Published by O'Reilly Media, Inc., 1005 Gravenstein Highway North, Sebastopol, CA 95472.

Editor: Laurel R. T. Ruma

Production Editor: Rachel Monaghan

Copyeditor: Audrey Doyle

Proofreader: Sumita Mukherji

Indexer: Julie Hawks

Interior Designer: Ron Bilodeau

Cover Designer: Monica Kamsvaag

Illustrator: Robert Romano

Printing History:

     November 2009: First Edition.

ISBN: 978-0-596-80660-6

[TM]

Gramma and Grumpa,
I am who I am today because of you guys.
Thank you.

Contents

CHAPTER 1

Introduction

Something strange is happening. Your advertising doesn't work anymore, at least not like it used to. You used to be able to buy some TV time or put an ad in a newspaper, but nowadays everyone has TiVo or a DVR and gets their news online. The conversations that took place under industrial broadcast media about your products happened in small groups, and their words disappeared as soon as they were spoken. Now the conversations happen in front of millions of people, and they're archived for years to come. Not only is your brand no longer the host, most of the time you're not even a welcome guest.

But it's not all doom and gloom. You don't have to try to outspend the biggest companies anymore; now you can outsmart them with viral videos. You don't have to spend thousands on sterile focus groups; you've got your market's pulse at your fingertips with quick Twitter searches. And you don't even have to do all the work yourself; the stuff that your fans create will blow you—and your competitors—away.

More than 250 million people are active Facebook users. More than 346 million people read blogs, and 184 million people are bloggers themselves. Twitter has more than 14 million registered users, and YouTube claims more than 100 million viewers per month. More consumers are connected than ever before, and every second your company is not engaging them in social media is a wasted opportunity. So, get on board.

What Is Social Media Marketing?

Social media is best defined in the context of the previous industrial media paradigm. Traditional media, such as television, newspapers, radio, and magazines, are one-way, static broadcast technologies. For instance, the magazine publisher is a large organization that distributes expensive content to consumers, while advertisers pay for the privilege of inserting their ads into that content. Or you're sitting down, watching

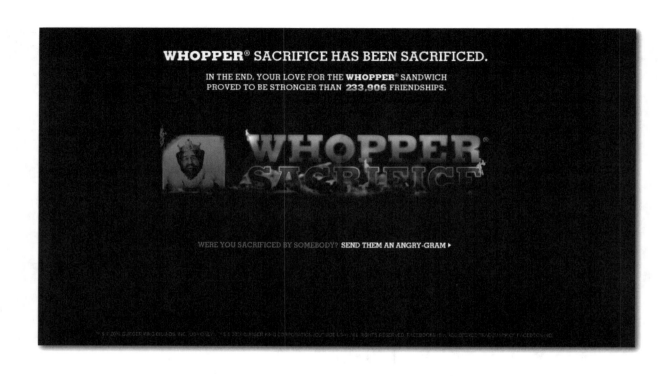

Figure 1-1. Burger King's Facebook application was so successful that it had to be shut down.

your favorite sitcom, and suddenly you're interrupted by commercials (luckily, you have a DVR, so you can fast-forward through them). If you disagree with something you read in the newspaper, you can't send the editorial staff instant feedback. And good luck connecting with your morning radio on-air personality.

New web technologies have made it easy for anyone to create—and, most importantly—distribute their own content. A blog post, tweet, or YouTube video can be produced and viewed by millions virtually for free. Advertisers don't have to pay publishers or distributors huge sums of money to embed their messages; now they can make their own interesting content that viewers will flock to.

Social media comes in many forms, but for our purposes, I'll focus on the eight most popular: blogs, microblogs (Twitter), social networks (Facebook, LinkedIn), media-sharing sites (YouTube, Flickr), social bookmarking and voting sites (Digg, Reddit), review sites (Yelp), forums, and virtual worlds (Second Life).

Big Brands and Social Media

IBM owns more than 100 different blogs, a dozen islands in the virtual world of Second Life, several official Twitter accounts, and a popular forum called developerWorks. It publishes a *machinima* series (a cartoon video made in Second Life) on YouTube, and several employees upload presentations to the media-sharing site SlideShare.

Dell has tapped the power of social media with its hugely popular IdeaStorm website, where users add ideas for new product lines and enhancements, vote them up or down, and comment on submissions. Because of the site, Dell has started to ship computers with Linux installed, and has added community support. Starbucks has also started to use this model to some success with its My Starbucks Idea site.

Burger King has made headlines time and time again with its innovative viral and social marketing campaigns, most recently with the "Whopper Sacrifice." The burger chain offered Facebook users a free Whopper coupon if they would "unfriend" 10 of their social network connections (see Figure 1-1).

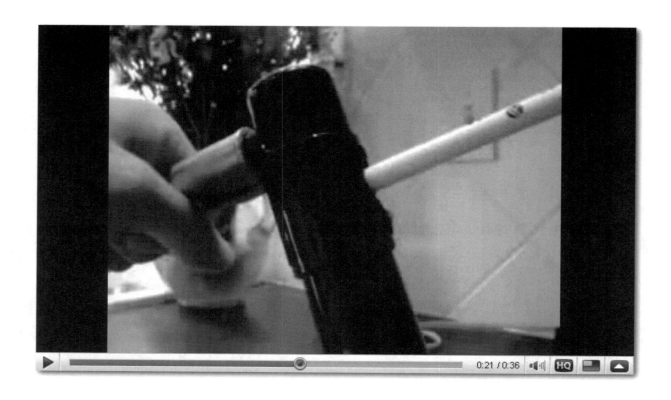

0:21 / 0:36

Figure 1-2. Viral videos demonstrated how to pick Kryptonite bike locks with only a Bic pen.

Cable giant Comcast has begun to salvage its tarnished reputation with a customer service outpost on Twitter led by Frank Eliason, Comcast's "Director of Digital Care," and his @comcastcares account. Whenever someone tweets negatively about the company—and that happens a lot—Frank jumps in to offer whatever help he can. This has led to some of the only positive press the brand has gotten in a long time. The shoe retailer Zappos, which most people already love, also has an awesome customer service presence on Twitter.

U.S. President Barack Obama has been called the first social media president, and a strong argument could be made for the label. As a candidate, he had one of the most popular Twitter accounts and Facebook pages, and his website contained a social media section where his supporters could create profiles and connect with each other. The campaign was also present on YouTube, Flickr, LinkedIn, MySpace, and Second Life.

Big brands have also faced embarrassment on social media. One example is shown in Figure 1-2. In another example, two Domino's Pizza employees posted a video to YouTube showing them defiling food that was to be delivered to customers. That video was watched more than 1 million times in the first few days, and was the subject of thousands of tweets.

Motrin released a commercial that offered its product as a solution to the pain women experience when carrying babies in harnesses attached to their torsos. A day later, a small but vocal group of mommy bloggers had made the commercial the most discussed topic on Twitter, mostly expressing outrage. These moms made critical videos and blog posts and called for a boycott of Motrin. Eventually, the company apologized and withdrew the commercial.

Figure 1-3. Blendtec's "Will It Blend" series was a social media hit.

Small Business and Social Media

As indicated previously, social media is a great equalizer: big brands can be outsmarted without making huge investments, and small brands can make big names for themselves.

Blendtec was a relatively unknown company selling $400 high-performance blenders. After seeing CEO Tom Dickson testing the machines by blending two-by-fours, Marketing Director George Wright had a brilliant idea for a series of viral videos. He started to blend everyday objects—glow sticks, iPhones, Rubik's Cubes, and television remote controls—and posted the videos to media-sharing sites such as YouTube (see Figure 1-3). The videos have now been watched more than 100 million times and have garnered the company a ton of press and buzz.

A small specialty baker in New Jersey, Pink Cake Box, leverages nearly every type of social media that exists to build a substantial brand. Employees write a blog that features images and videos of their unique cakes. They post the photos to Flickr and the videos to the company's YouTube channel. Pink Cake Box has more than 1,300 followers on Twitter, and more than 1,400 fans on Facebook.

The software startup I work for, HubSpot, has invested a lot of energy in social media marketing with some success. Our blog has more than 19,000 subscribers (fueled by appearances on Digg, Reddit, and StumbleUpon), our company Twitter account has more than 16,000 followers, our LinkedIn group has more than 34,000 members, and our Facebook page has more than 6,000 fans. We've launched a marketing forum, and have a lot of fun making amusing (and sometimes serious) videos for YouTube.

Social Media and You

Whether you are part of a small, medium, or giant business, or are an individual entrepreneur, your customers are using social media, and there's no reason you shouldn't be, too. It costs almost nothing, it's easy to get started, and it can have an enormous financial impact on your business.

This book will teach you everything you need to know to pick the right tools and get started. While writing this book, I spoke with some of the most brilliant social media pioneers, including people from Flickr, Yelp, Mashable, WebmasterWorld, Second Life, and Scout Labs. They shared their wisdom on how you can—and should—be working with social media.

Your customers and your competition are already involved in social media. Why aren't you?

CHAPTER 2
Blogging

Introduction

A *blog* is a type of content management system (CMS) that makes it easy for anyone to publish short articles called *posts*. Blog software provides a variety of social features, including comments, blogrolls, trackbacks, and subscriptions that make it perfect for marketing purposes. Blogs make great hubs for your other social media marketing efforts, as they can be integrated with nearly every other tool and platform.

Every company with a website should have a blog that speaks to its current and potential customers as real people. Blogs are not the right place for corporate-speak press releases; blogs should be conversational in tone. Every time your company does something new or cool, write a quick post about it. Blog about your take on news that affects your industry. If a related blog posts something you think is particularly interesting or incorrect, link to it and add your thoughts.

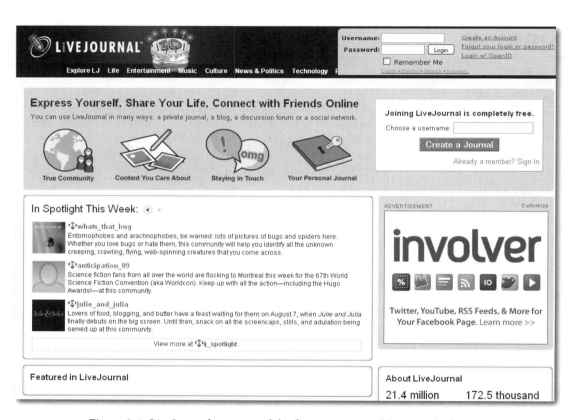

Figure 2-1. LiveJournal was one of the first easy-to-use blogging platforms.

History

People have been keeping journals for thousands of years (an example is Roman Emperor Marcus Aurelius), and have been able to write them online since 1994. Justin Hall, a student at Swarthmore College, was one of the first web diarists when he started writing about video games and gaming conventions in the mid-1990s. Originally, these journals were nothing more than parts of regular sites that were updated regularly, by hand, in HTML. The technical knowledge this required prevented the average person from starting an online diary.

In December 1997, the word *weblog*, a combination of the words *web* and *log*, was born; eventually, *weblog* was shortened to just *blog*. This is probably one of the least understood and most ridiculed words on the Web; I've heard people who should know better explain it as having come from a bunch of ridiculous origins (including *business log*).

Blogging didn't start to blossom until 1999, when LiveJournal (see Figure 2-1) and Blogger were launched, the latter by Evan Williams (who went on to create Twitter). Users could sign up to one of these two sites and start their own blogs for free, with no technical ability required. By the end of 2008, 346 million people were reading blogs, and 184 million had started one of their own.

SOCIAL NETWORKING GOD: 350+ Social Networking Sites

October 23rd, 2007 | by Daksh Sharma   200 Comments

SOCIAL NETWORKING
GOD
350+ SOCIAL NETWORKING SITES

NEW: Sponsor Mashable Lists. Click here for sponsor info.

One of the main topics here at Mashable ⊟ has always been social networking. In the past several years, some networks have thrived, some vanished, while hundreds of new ones appeared. It has become a huge area to follow, and this article illustrates this well: a collection of over 350 social networking sites, all of which were covered in one way or another here at Mashable. We hope to have created an extensive and useful resource for anyone interested in social networking. Enjoy.

Feel free to add more apps in the comments. And don't forget to subscribe to Mashable for the latest web news and resources.

Books

booksconnect
CONNECTING THE BOOK COMMUNITY

Americabookshelf.com – One of the largest book exchange clubs across the US.

Figure 2-2. Mashable's "God List" posts took a long time to make, but resulted in thousands of visitors and links.

Protocol

Blogging platforms all share some common traits and features that make them blogs. In this section, I'll explain some of these characteristics and show you how you can use them for marketing.

Posts

Blogs are made of posts. A post can be any length, from 100 or 200 words to many pages, but to be most effective, it should always stick to a single topic.

Mashable is one of the five most popular blogs on the Web, according to Technorati, and is the leader in the social media niche. I asked founder Pete Cashmore for his advice on blogging, and he said the most important element of a successful blog is consistent, quality posts. Pete also suggested setting a goal, such as one post per day for a year, and then sticking to it.

In the early days of Mashable, Pete had a lot of success with huge collections of links to tools and resources called "God List" posts (see Figure 2-2). These took an enormous amount of time to create, but once they were written, they drew incoming links and traffic for years. Pete emphasized that if you're writing long posts, you need to structure them in such a way that they include "scannable" items such as subheadings, lists, and images.

On the opposite end of the spectrum is the short-form content that is often used to publish news and events. If you've committed to publishing regularly, quick posts of a couple hundred words can help you feel like you've accomplished something when writing feels like a chore. Pete recommends posting a mix of short and long posts.

Figure 2-3. This is an example of a permalink page.

5 Responses to "Why Jokes Go Viral"

1. **Mark Lee** Says:
   July 15th, 2009 at 10:54 am

   Useful analysis Dan.
   Thanks for that.
   I may well go back and check which of the automatically tweeted items from my accountant jokes and fun blog have been retweeted. I'd be surprised if there's a discernible pattern, but I won't know until I check.

2. **Ankesh Kothari** Says:
   July 15th, 2009 at 11:02 am

   Good stuff as usual Dan.

   I think jokes spread because they help build a deeper connection between folks quicker. Nothing brings people together than shared laughter.

   The cognitive dissonance is what makes a joke poignant. The disconnect and unexpectedness is what makes it funny. And we spread it because thats what helps us connect with other folks.

3. **Timi Stoop-Alcala** Says:
   July 15th, 2009 at 5:40 pm

   Love the subject. Reminds me of a historical event in the Philippines where jokes (coupled with sms technology) played a great role in the impeachment and imprisonment of the president.

   Jan 17-21 saw the unfolding of 'Edsa Dos' (Edsa 2 - Edsa's the name of a major highway where the first 'People Power Revolution' took place, and this time around, where the protesters against then President Joseph Estrada converged). Estrada or 'Erap' was a former actor-turned-Mayor who was elected President. He was exposed to have received millions of pesos from the operations of an illegal numbers game.

Figure 2-4. The comment section on a blog is a great place to build a community and get feedback.

Permalinks

Each post on a blog can be seen in a variety of places, including the home page, category page, and archive pages. These pages are dynamically generated, and as new posts are added old ones are buried. The one place where you can always find a specific post (and only that one post) is on its *permalink* page (see Figure 2-3). These permanent links are what you'll be promoting on Twitter or social news sites. Good blogging software should allow the URLs of these pages to be short and clean, without question marks or ampersands. Clean URLs also make it easier for search engines and users to consume your content.

Comments

Most blogs have a section below each post where users can leave comments (see Figure 2-4). This comment section is a great place to build a community and get feedback. Make an effort to respond to as many comments as you can, especially when your blog is first starting out. If someone leaves a negative comment that is based on a legitimate concern, respond to it, don't delete it. But if someone is being disruptive or offensive, feel free to delete the comment; this is your blog.

Spend some time each day posting thoughtful comments on other blogs in your industry. Pick a few well-known blogs that are relevant to yours, and become a valuable member of their communities. This is a great way to get connected to other people in your space, but you'll need to balance this with the time you spend creating your own quality content, as content trumps comments.

Because most blog platforms allow commenters to include a link to their sites, comments have become a favorite target of spammers. Your software should have a mechanism—such as a CAPTCHA—in place to prevent this. And when you're commenting on someone else's site, use your real name and leave out unnecessary links so that other bloggers don't think you're a spammer.

Figure 2-5. Thousands of free themes are available on the WordPress site.

Figure 2-6. Monthly archives are popular on old blogs.

Popular comment sections are similar to forums, so check out Chapter 8 for a better understanding of how to grow and manage your own community as well as engage in other blogs.

Themes

Most blogging software allows you to customize the look of your site through the use of *themes*. Themes are collections of CSS, HTML, and graphics that can be applied to any blog using a specific platform. For example, a WordPress theme will work on any WordPress blog and will change the look of the content that is already there (see Figure 2-5).

Thousands of free and paid themes are available on the Web, but many of the most popular blogs have unique themes designed for them. The look of your site is vital to establishing an image of authority; you'll have a harder time gaining your readers' trust if you have an amateurish-looking or extremely common theme.

Archive and Category Pages

Posts are displayed in reverse chronological order; typically, only the most recent 10 or 20 posts will appear on a blog's home page. To make older posts easier to find, most blogging software includes archive pages where users can browse through past content by day, week, or month. Figure 2-6 shows an example of a monthly archive.

To organize posts by topic, rather than simply chronology, you should label each post with one or more categories or tags. Users can then browse your content by topic through the use of category pages, which are provided in most platforms (see Figure 2-7). When you're creating the list of categories for your site, think of a first-time user to your site: what topics would he want to navigate to first?

saves it for today? Tomorrow, there's another emergency, and yesterday's dollar is gone. So you need another dollar. Two billion people, two billion dollars. Every day. Today, tomorrow, the day after that. It's an endless emergency, and it never gets better.

That's where patient capital comes in. It starts with this belief:

The difference between being one penny behind and one penny ahead is profound.

If you're one penny behind, then every day you fall further back. Every day, the emergencies get worse, the stress gets worse, your ability to survive (never mind thrive) gets worse.

Ahead and behind

If you're one penny ahead, though, just a penny, then every day you build a reserve, every day you are able to invest in productivity or peace of mind, and soon you are two pennies or a dollar or five dollars a day ahead. And then you can send your daughter to college. And then you can buy something from the merchant next door. And then you can plant a better crop. And then you have a stake in the community, and then the world changes.

So, how to create this micro surplus? How to prime the pump of the system to improve productivity enough that things get better?

Markets.

When two people trade, both win. No one buys a bar a soap unless the money they're spending for the soap is worth less to them than the soap itself.

When someone in poverty buys a device that improves productivity, the device pays for itself (if it didn't, they wouldn't buy it.) So a drip irrigation system, for example, may pay off by creating two or three harvests a year instead of one.

What does that do for the family that buys it? Well, if you have one harvest a

Figure 2-7. Category pages are a feature that is included in most blogging software.

Blogrolls

A *blogroll* is a list of links to other blogs that many bloggers have in their sidebars as recommendations. The understood meaning is that these are the sites the blogger reads regularly, but most modern bloggers read many more blogs than they can fit in their blogroll. A good way to use your blogroll is to link to popular sites in your niche in the hopes that those bloggers and their audience will notice and read your blog. But don't go crazy; try to keep your blogroll at around 30 links.

Links

Links are the currency of blogging. Incoming links send traffic, of course, but they also help a site rank better in search engines. Because links are so highly sought after, most bloggers pay close attention to who is linking to them with blog search engines such as Technorati and Google Blog Search. In the blogosphere, links are a form of communication: if you link to me, I'll see it in a few hours and will probably read what you said about me. If I like it—or dislike it enough—I may respond. Either way, I now know your site.

Trackbacks and Pingbacks

Most blogging software sends trackbacks or pingbacks when you link to another blog. Simply put, these are notifications from one blog to another that the sender has pointed a link at the receiver. These were very popular when they were first invented, but they have since become overrun with spam, so most bloggers pay more attention to traffic or blog search engines.

Figure 2-8. Here's an example of the TweetMeme button
on a blog post.

Figure 2-9. Readers can subscribe to a blog
via RSS or email.

The TweetMeme Button

TweetMeme.com offers a small piece of JavaScript that you can copy and paste into your posts that will show your readers how many people have tweeted about it as well as allow them easy, one-click retweeting of your content. Guy Kawasaki has called this the most important button on the Web. There are plug-ins for WordPress, TypePad, and Blogger that simplify integration. Figure 2-8 shows the TweetMeme button on a blog post.

Subscriptions

Blog software gives you the powerful ability to syndicate your content using popular formats such as RSS and Atom. These standards are designed to allow people to read your content—as well as their other favorite blogs—in a piece of software known as a *feed reader*. Good blogging software makes this easy by providing people with a simple button to click to add your blog to their subscription lists. People who subscribe won't come to your site every time they read your content, but once they have subscribed to your feed, they will read most or all of your posts. Similar software, such as FeedBurner, converts your feeds into an email format so that your visitors can receive your posts in their inboxes (see Figure 2-9).

If your intended audience is tech savvy, you should emphasize feed-based subscriptions. If not, be sure to offer an email subscription option. Either way, display links to both methods prominently in your theme, as they will result in repeat visitors.

Platforms

Blogs can be set up on a variety of platforms. This section will introduce the two types of platforms available, and detail some of the features of the specific choices.

Figure 2-10. WordPress is robust, free, and easy to use once it's set up.

Hosted Versus Self-Hosted

Blogging software falls into one of two varieties: hosted or self-hosted. *Hosted software*, such as LiveJournal, resides on a server owned by the organization that maintains the code. Many hosted solutions will give you a URL to use, such as *http://<example>.wordpress.com*. *Self-hosted software* is run on your own server. Self-hosted platforms require installation and configuration, but once they are set up they're completely under your control. Blogs running self-hosted software are located on a domain owned solely by you, as opposed to the shared domains often used by hosted blogs. Hosted software is often easier for new bloggers to get started on, but for best results your blog should appear on your own domain. Some hosted blog systems allow you to use your own domain; take advantage of this if you can.

Most popular blogs today use self-hosted software, and chances are good that you'll need help installing, designing, configuring, and maintaining your blog to get it running to your needs. Rather than hire a dedicated in-house person to manage this for you, you should look for technical help in your industry or location. Mashable's Pete Cashmore recommends finding a firm or individual who would like to increase her exposure in your niche, and offering a trade of advertising space on your site and blog for free or discounted services.

WordPress

WordPress is the most well-known and widely used blogging software, as well as my personal favorite. It is free, is open source, and has a robust community of developers and designers who've built thousands of plug-ins and themes for it, making it the most customizable platform available. Once WordPress is installed and set up, it is also one of the easiest to use, but as I mentioned before, you may need some technical help to get it up and running (see Figure 2-10).

Figure 2-11. TypePad is similar to WordPress, but features free and paid versions.

Figure 2-12. Blogger is popular, free, and easy to use, but it lacks some features.

Wordpress.com also offers a hosted version of WordPress software that can be used for free. If you're thinking of using WordPress for your blog, Pete suggests that you try a free account to see whether you like the platform.

Movable Type

Many of the most high-traffic blogs on the Web use Movable Type. In the past few years, Movable Type has shifted to an open source model and now has great support for multiple blogs, but it is not as easy to use as WordPress. The most popular paid, hosted platform on the Web is TypePad (see Figure 2-11). Based on Movable Type software and owned by the same company (Six Apart), TypePad is simpler to use than the self-hosted version and includes a few additional features. Some sites running on TypePad use domains such as *http://<example>.typepad.com*, whereas others use their own domains.

Blogger

One of the earliest blogging platforms, Blogger is hosted software (see Figure 2-12); most sites using it appear on URLs such as *http://<example>.blogspot.com*. It is very easy to use, but it lacks many of the features available in other platform solutions. It is a popular choice for new bloggers creating their first sites.

HubSpot

HubSpot (the company I work for) sells a set of tools, including a blogging package. This paid, hosted service allows your blog to appear on your domain and includes features for companies that want to integrate their blogs with their lead-tracking and marketing analytics.

Figure 2-13. Posts breaking important news are a sure hit.

Content Strategies

Pete Cashmore told me he thinks the most important choice you'll make when starting your blog is to choose a topic you can dominate—avoid overcrowded areas that have a bunch of popular blogs, if you can. Regardless of the size of your niche, however, blogging is a personal medium, so focus on bringing your own voice and unique point of view forward. Local businesses also have the option of blogging about a topic in a geographic area; if you can't be the biggest law blog, you can be the biggest law blog in Minneapolis.

Once you've picked your niche, you'll need to put in the work. Mix up the kind of content you post, and focus on types of content that are known to drive traffic and links. In the following sections, I describe a few kinds of content that often do very well for new blogs and are easy ways to become accustomed to the medium.

News

The most popular kind of content you'll probably ever be able to publish is breaking, exclusive news (for an example, see Figure 2-13). The problem, of course, is that breaking news is pretty hard to come by. The best way to come into this kind of information is to establish real-world connections with people working in your industry. Of course, sometimes you may happen upon such information just by being in the right place at the right time: always keep your eyes and ears open.

When you do hear about something you can write about, act fast. There is very little benefit to publishing second or third. Get as many details and as much media—photos, videos, or audio—as you can, and then click Publish.

Research | Tools | Portfolio | Bio | Contact

Reports on surveys and studies I've conducted.

Social, viral and search tools.

A few examples of the work I've done recently.

A little bit about me.

Email mail me to see what I can do for you.

"The Social Media & Viral Marketing Scientist"

10 Symptoms of Highly Viral WordPress Themes

Posted on Oct 14th, 2008 | 12 comments so far.

235
diggs

dugg!

Blogs are my favorite CMS for "going viral." Cheap, easy, expandable, everything you could want. But when you're launching a blog and your goal is going to be lots of social media and viral traffic, you'll need to make sure you pick the right theme. Here are a list of 10 things your theme must have to "go viral."

1. Social Buttons

Most blogs these days have the sociable plugin, so that there is a list of social sites at the bottom of every post that allow readers to submit and vote on the post. For real traction, you need to do better than these teeny little buttons. Put big, honkin' voting buttons on every post on your site. For instance, I really like what Brent Csutoras does on his blog.

2. Images and Video

Experienced social media marketers will tell you that you should always add images and if you can, video to a post to help it do better on social voting sites. So you should make sure that your theme's central content area is wide enough to handle high-quality images and embedded videos. I would typically recommend at least 500px wide.

Hi, I'm Dan Zarrella.

I'm a social & viral marketing scientist; read my bio here. To get an idea of what I do, check out my portfolio, tools, and research reports. If you like my stuff, subscribe to my feed, follow me on Twitter or email me.

Follow me on **Twitter**

Subscribe to my **Blog**

Get my posts sent to your inbox by entering your email below:

Figure 2-14. List posts are easy to make and read.

Lists

Readers find content that is broken into short bits easier to read than long blocks of boring text. Lists are a perfect example of this (see Figure 2-14). Rank the 10 best of a certain thing or the 10 worst. Find the 10 most expensive or the 10 weirdest. If you can, add an image or video example for each item, and list them in descending order.

How-To's

Chances are good that you know how to do something others don't. So, write a tutorial about it. Add video or images, and break the steps down into a numbered list. The simpler you can make a seemingly complex task, the more your readers will thank you for it. Useful information is one of the most commonly shared types of content on the Web, so posts such as these are known to spread like wildfire.

Controversy

First, a word of caution: anyone can stir the pot and inflame tempers. If you don't have a good argument, chances are you'll catch serious backlash if your attempt at creating baseless controversy works. That being said, if you can disprove or make a strong case against something that everyone likes, or if you are in favor of something that everyone dislikes, you may have a grand slam of a post on your hands. Don't maker personal attacks, and do stick to your facts. And, unless you want to be known as the person who is always looking for a scrap, don't make this a habit.

Building an Audience

You've got a blog set up and you've picked a niche. You've written a few solid posts, and you're ready to roll, but no one's subscribing or commenting. What's missing? (Besides readers, of course.) You need to have an understanding of where these readers originate. Blogs are best thought of as hubs for your social media marketing efforts, and the other chapters in this book will teach you how to reach out to various communities; your blog is a good place to point the people you meet. Hopefully, you're among your target demographic, so ask yourself: where do you hang out online?

A crucial aspect of building an audience is connecting with other bloggers in your niche. I've already described two easy ways to do this: links and commenting. But you can also get to know them on other social sites, especially Twitter. I'm much more likely to link to you from my blog if I've had a conversation or two with you before.

Takeaway Tips

- Every company should have a blog, and it should be the center of your social marketing efforts.

- Pick a niche you can own, stay away from crowded areas, and bring your unique voice.

- Get a good design. Without one, you'll find it hard to be taken seriously.

- Establish a consistent habit of regular posting, and stick to it.

- Get to know other bloggers in your industry and become a valuable part of their community to increase the visibility of your own blog.

- Mix up content types and add multimedia.

CHAPTER 3

Twitter and Microblogging

Introduction

Microblogging is a form of blogging that limits the size of each post; for instance, Twitter updates can contain only 140 characters. This limitation has spawned a set of features, protocols, and behavior that are entirely unique to the medium. Twitter started to take off in terms of popularity in the first half of 2009 as a result of high-profile celebrity members and a mention on *Oprah*, and now it has become more mainstream than other similar social media tools.

Most companies should be on Twitter; it's easy, requires very little investment of time, and can quickly prove worthwhile in increased buzz, sales, and consumer insight. You can use Twitter to announce offers or events, promote new blog posts, or keep your readers in the know with links to important news stories.

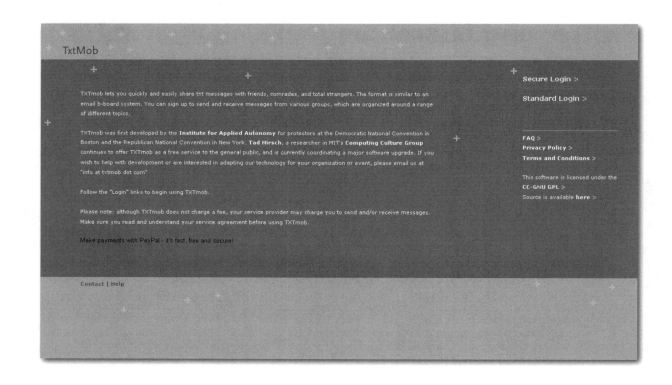

Figure 3-1. TXTmob was an early inspiration for Twitter.

History

In 2004, a group of technologists and activists created an organizational tool called TXTmob that allowed protesters at the 2004 political conventions to communicate through short text messages that were widely broadcast through SMS to the cell phones of a group of people.

Two years later, web-based podcasting startup Odeo was failing, and its board members decided to spend a day in small groups brainstorming other ideas to "reboot" their business. One group met on a playground; sitting on top of a slide, group member Jack Dorsey proposed an SMS broadcast system similar to and inspired by TXTmob (see Figure 3-1).

And thus Twitter was built in March 2006. The following year, at the South by Southwest Interactive conference, the service reached its first tipping point when usage spiked from 20,000 messages per day to 60,000 messages per day; thousands of conference-goers used Twitter to find one another and to comment on panel sessions in real time. As of May 2007, 111 microblogging systems were in operation, but Twitter is by far the most popular today.

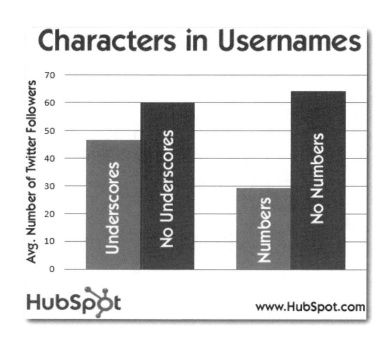

Figure 3-2. Numbers and underscores in your username typically lead to fewer followers.

Protocol

The microblog is a type of social media site, and although Twitter is the dominant flavor currently, this may not always be true. I'll introduce you to the basic elements of the microblogging format in this section.

Account

On Twitter, personal and company accounts exist alongside a wide range of fictional and inanimate accounts. Compared to other social media sites, Twitter corporate accounts enjoy greater acceptance. It's OK to set up an account for your company, as well as an account for yourself individually. In fact, my research has shown that "official brand" Twitter accounts are often highly followed.

Many successful Twitterers use their first and last names joined together into one long string as their *handles* (the Twitter term for usernames). Unfortunately, some people (especially those with common names) cannot do this because their first and last names have already been taken, so they resort to a name with underscores and numbers. This means that because I already use @danzarrella as my Twitter handle, the next Dan Zarrella to join Twitter might end up picking @dan_zarrella. This is a bad idea, particularly if you're trying to build an account with lots of followers, as my research has shown that users with underscores and numbers in their names have fewer followers on average (see Figure 3-2).

Avatar

When people read your *tweets* (Twitter lingo for *posts*), the tweets will be shown next to a small image you have uploaded to Twitter. In most places, this image is a 48×48 pixel square. This picture is how most people will recognize tweets as being yours, so use something that stands out and don't change it frequently. For personal accounts, a good-quality head shot is the best option; for company accounts, your logo will work, as long as it is recognizable in a small size.

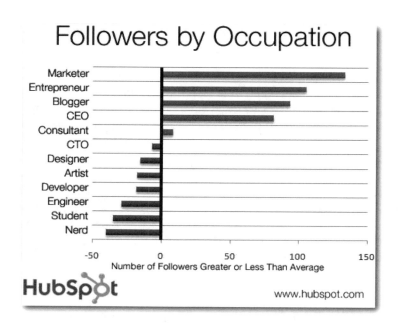

Figure 3-3. Certain titles in your bio tend to lead to more followers.

Bio

When you're creating your account, you'll have 160 characters in a section called "Bio" to explain who you are. This takes very little time to write, and research has shown that accounts with bios have far more followers on average than accounts without bios.

I explored what relationship the content of a user's bio has on the number of followers the user has. Marketers and entrepreneurs tend to have more followers than the rest, as do accounts labeled *official*, *founder*, *expert*, and *author*. I also looked at the relationship between follower numbers and gender and family roles. I found that spouses and parents have more followers than the average, whereas people who refer to themselves by the somewhat diminutive terms *boy* and *girl* have fewer followers. While looking over the large list of commonly occurring words, I noticed that lots of people use emoticons in their bios and nearly all of them have a negative relationship with follower numbers. Figure 3-3 shows a chart of the results of my research on followers by occupation.

Background

Twitter gives you the ability to design and upload a custom background image for your account page. Some users take advantage of this and add lots of extra information about themselves, including other social sites where they can be found. Since these background images are not clickable, they can be frustrating, especially to new users. The best custom background image to use is one that shows your company's colors or logo to reinforce your brand image.

Figure 3-4. Any tweet containing your username will be shown on your Replies page.

Following

When you *follow* someone on Twitter, you'll see her tweets in her timeline, and if she follows you back, she'll see yours. The number of followers you have is the number of people who will potentially be exposed to your tweets, so to increase your reach, you should try to get more followers.

It's not a bad idea for those on corporate accounts to follow everyone who follows you; to do otherwise may make your brand appear aloof. Several web-based services will do this for you. Those on personal accounts, on the other hand, should not feel obligated to do this. In fact, my research shows that Twitterers who have more followers than people they are following tend to have larger audiences.

When you're first getting started, you can use Twitter's Find People feature to locate people you already communicate with via email to follow. You should also use Twitter search to find people talking about your company, industry, and interests, and make sure to follow them as well.

Tweeting

The core of Twitter is the tweet: a 140-character or less text message posted to Twitter. The word *tweet* can be used as a noun, as in, "Have you seen this tweet?" and as a verb, as in, "Please tweet this."

Twitter was originally intended as a way for people to answer the question "What are you doing?" And although some people post real-time updates about their lives, it is far more useful for marketers to tweet about new content, offers, and news, as well as respond to questions from other users.

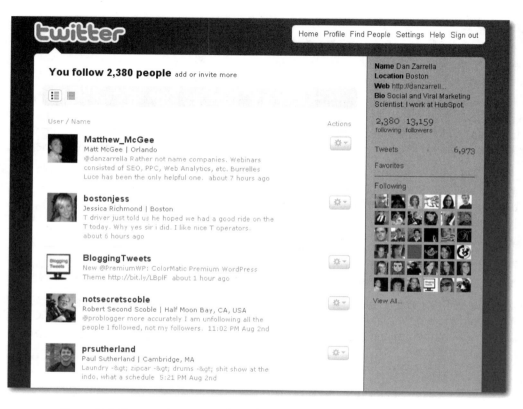

Figure 3-5. You see the tweets of people you follow in your friends timeline.

Replies

Conversations on Twitter are conducted through "@" replies. When you include "@*username*" in a tweet, where *username* is the name of the person you're talking to, it will show up in that person's Replies tab. Likewise, you can see who has mentioned your name by clicking on the "@*username*" link when you're logged in to Twitter (seen earlier in Figure 3-4). If a tweet starts with an @ sign, only people who are following both you and the person you tweeted will see it in their *friends timeline* (see Figure 3-5). Replies such as this are still public if someone views your Twitter stream specifically or uses Twitter search.

To seem approachable and genuinely interested in conversation, you should respond to as many messages as you can. A good way to keep an eye on this is to look at your stream and count the percentage of your tweets that are replies versus those that are not.

Retweets

Retweets are the most powerful mechanisms for marketers on Twitter. If I tweet something, my followers will see it. If you are following me and you copy and paste what I've posted verbatim to your Twitter stream, your followers will see it, and one of them may also retweet it. This way, a message can spread virally through Twitter, reaching tens or hundreds of times as many people as it would if only a single person tweeted it (see Figure 3-6). It can be useful to ask your followers to retweet something you've posted (but do so in moderation).

The popular Twitter client TweetDeck has a retweet button, so it has defined a kind of de facto standard format for retweeting. Many people also add their own thoughts at the end of a retweet. The most commonly accepted retweet format is as follows:

```
RT @username: Original Tweet (Your Take)
```

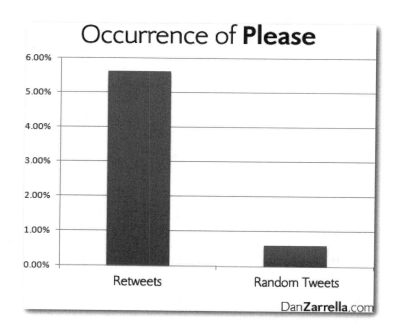

Figure 3-6. Asking for retweets works.

A Twitter client is a piece of software that makes it easier to use Twitter. I will discuss this in more detail in the Clients section on page 51.

Retweeting was not invented by the Twitter creators; rather, it was popularized by Twitter users. As such, there is no single set of guidelines for how to retweet correctly, but here are a few points to get you started:

- Do not start the retweet with an @ sign.

- Try to credit at least the original user who posted the tweet. If you have room, also try to credit the person whose retweet you saw.

- The most common retweet format is *RT: @username*. Typically, this is reserved for the original poster.

- If the original tweet included a call to action (such as "please retweet"), try to keep that in your retweet.

- If the original tweet has a link in it, keep it there.

- Try to keep as much of the original tweet intact as possible, but it is acceptable to add your take on it (especially at the end, in parentheses).

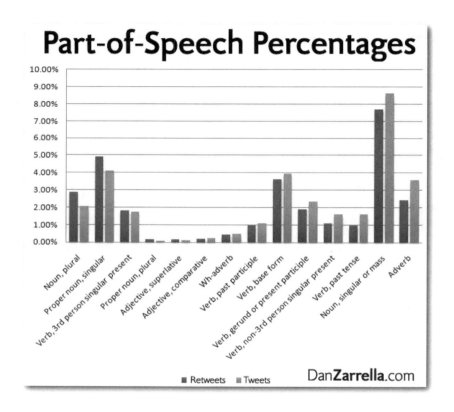

Figure 3-7. Retweets are noun heavy and use third-person verbs.

Because of the power of a retweet, I've done extensive research to understand what types of tweets get retweeted most often. At the time of this writing, it is impossible to predict what will definitely get retweeted, but I've found a few characteristics that can lead to more retweets:

- Between 11:00 a.m. and 6:00 p.m. EST is the most popular time for retweeting.

- Asking for the retweet—by explicitly saying "please retweet"—sounds cheesy, but it works. But don't ask every time.

- Most retweets contain a link, many more than nonretweet updates.

- Retweets tend to contain more nouns and third-person verbs than nonretweets (see Figure 3-7).

- Talking about yourself won't get you retweeted very much.

- Posting about social media, Twitter itself in particular, will get you retweets.

Direct Messages

Direct messages (DMs) are the private messages of Twitter. If I'm following you, you can DM me, and only if you're following me back can I DM you in reply. Twitter's default behavior sends DM notifications to the recipient's email inbox, so treat DMs as you would treat normal email: no spamming.

Several web tools are available to set up what are called *auto-DMs*, where your account automatically sends a DM to everyone who follows you, typically with a greeting and a link to your site. Most Twitter users consider auto-DMs annoying, so avoid them.

Figure 3-8. Trending topics are now displayed on the main Twitter interface.

Trending Topics

Twitter has developed an algorithm that tracks mentions of words and phrases up to three words long, and highlights those that are the most talked about at any given point in time. You'll find this as a top 10 list in the righthand column of your Twitter page. Popular events, news, and memes generally make up these trending topics (see Figure 3-8). If your company's name appears in this list, it can drive a significant amount of buzz and awareness, but the actual number of new followers or traffic produced is often surprisingly low. A better way to use trending topics is as a barometer for what the Twitter community is currently interested in and talking about.

Hashtags

To connect ideas and conversations into a cohesive stream in Twitter's otherwise free-form landscape, people often use *hashtags*. Simply a word preceded by the pound or number sign (#), a hashtag is used to indicate that a certain tweet is about the same topic as every other tweet using the same tag. In many Twitter clients, clicking on a hashtag will bring you to a search for that term. In the Twitter search results, you can see the entire conversation that used that tag in real time.

Popular uses of hashtags include social media campaigns, news, political events and issues, and conferences. They help unify topics that might be discussed with a handful of different words. Tweets about the Boston Red Sox, for example, could include the words *Bo Sox*, *Sox*, or *Red Sox*; using *#RedSox* keeps it all organized.

Figure 3-9. To share URLs, you should shorten them with a URL shortening service.

Shortened URLs

Since each tweet has a 140-character limit, space is at a premium. URLs tend to be fairly long and take up too much space in a tweet, so a handful of services have been developed that allow you to shorten links. With these services, you enter a URL, and then the service returns a much shorter version that redirects visitors to the original address (see Figure 3-9).

These shorteners take one of two forms: pre-Twitter and post-Twitter. Pre-Twitter shorteners, such as Tinyurl.com, typically produce longer URLs than other services and do not allow you to count the number of times your link has been clicked. Most post-Twitter services, such as bit.ly, do track clicks. Here's a brief explanation of a handful of URL-shortening services:

TinyURL (*http://TinyURL.com*)

> One of the earliest URL shorteners, TinyURL is still the most popular. It does not offer click tracking, but it does have a bookmarklet for easy shortening.

Bit.ly (*http://bit.ly*)

> The default shortener for Twitter.com and TweetDeck, bit.ly allows you to create an account and analyze the number of clicks your short URLs are getting.

Ow.ly (*http://ow.ly*)

> Ow.ly is integrated into the HootSuite application, which allows click tracking as well as tweet scheduling.

Figure 3-10. TweetDeck allows you to manage lots of followers and friends.

Clients

Twitter was originally built for messaging from mobile phones via SMS, and although the website is the most popular Twitter interface right now, hundreds of third-party applications are available that add more features for tweeting. Some of these applications make it easier to manage lots of followers or to update your tweets from your phone. Here is a sampling of these applications:

TweetDeck

> My favorite Twitter client and the most popular application, TweetDeck (see Figure 3-10) offers features that simplify managing lots of followers, such as groups, searches, and Twitpic integration. TweetDeck is free and runs on Adobe Air, so you can use it on Mac, Windows, and many types of Linux machines.

Tweetie

> Tweetie is an application for Macs and iPhones. The Mac software has a free version that is ad supported, as well as a paid version. The iPhone software can be purchased through Apple's App Store. Both the Mac and iPhone versions can handle multiple accounts and support threaded reply and direct message conversations.

Twhirl

> Twhirl is another Adobe Air desktop application. It includes a spellchecker and is designed to be very simple and easy to use, making it a good client for new Twitter users. Power users may find it too limiting, however.

HootSuite

> HootSuite is my favorite web-based Twitter client. It allows teams to manage single (or multiple) accounts, and it includes functionality to schedule tweets to be posted in the future. It is integrated with the Ow.ly URL shortener, and offers extensive analytics regarding clicks and mentions of your brand.

Takeaway Tips

- Microblogging is a quick and easy way to get into social media and promote your content.

- Set up your account for optimal following and tweeting, with a good avatar and an optimized bio.

- Follow people you already know, and search for people who tweet about your interests and follow them.

- Twitter is all about two-way conversations; engage with people, don't just broadcast.

- Ask for retweets (politely) to get them.

- Monitor the trending topics list to check the pulse of the Twittersphere.

- Use Twitter clients that help you manage your account on your desktop and mobile device.

CHAPTER 4

Social Networking

Introduction

A social network is a website where people connect with friends, both those they know offline and those who are online-only buddies. Social networking sites are a hot topic for marketers, as they present a number of opportunities for interacting with customers, including via plug-in applications, groups, and fan pages.

Each social network presents its own possibilities and challenges. Users of individual sites have different expectations of commercial behavior. In this chapter, I'll introduce you to the three most popular networks and their unique features.

History

The roots of online social networking can be traced to the 1980s bulletin board systems (BBSs). These systems allowed users to log in—through very slow connections—to share software and data as well as send private messages and post to public message boards. Due to the high cost of the long distance calls that would be required to access BBSs in other parts of the world, most of these were very local communities.

*Figure 4-1. Friendster was one of the first popular
social networking sites.*

The late '80s and early '90s saw the rise of the desktop applications CompuServe, Prodigy, and AOL. Far more feature-rich than BBSs, these systems allowed users to connect to the Internet and create personal profiles, post events, chat, and send public and private messages.

As the World Wide Web grew in popularity, social networking moved to web-based applications. The first wave was built for specific functions or audiences. In 1995, Classmates.com and Match.com were created; both remain fairly popular sites in their niche. In 1999, more targeted networks were launched, including BlackPlanet.com, MiGente.com, and AsianAvenue.com.

The modern era of social networks began in 2002, when Jonathan Abrams launched Friendster (see Figure 4-1). Inspired by Match.com, Abrams wanted Friendster to be a dating site that wasn't about dating. In what many consider to be one of the biggest financial mistakes in recent history, Friendster rejected a $30 million buyout offer from search giant Google.

In 2003, several employees of a marketing company now known as Intermix Media—which was later sued by then–New York Attorney General Elliot Spitzer for making malicious spyware applications—duplicated the core functionality of Friendster and launched MySpace. Initially powered by Intermix Media's large email lists, MySpace quickly became a leader among social networking sites. Thanks to its customizable user profiles and its focus on music, MySpace had a cooler image than its somewhat stodgy rival, Friendster. In July 2005, News Corporation purchased MySpace and its parent company for $580 million.

Then, in October 2003, a Harvard sophomore named Mark Zuckerberg hacked into the university's private dorm ID database and created Facemash, a site that let students compare two ID photos to select the more attractive one. Narrowly avoiding legal action, Zuckerberg went on to create "The Facebook," a social network that began as an exclusive site for Harvard students. Slowly the site allowed other colleges to join—initially only Ivy League schools, and then other colleges, and then, eventually, high schools. Finally, in 2006, anyone with an email address could sign up.

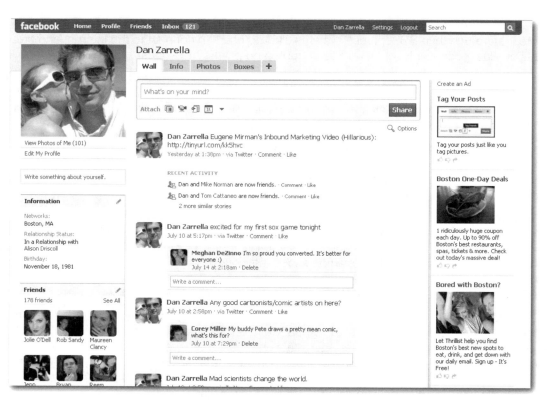

Figure 4-2. Here is my Facebook profile.

Sometime between April 2008 and February 2009, Facebook overtook the long-standing king, MySpace, as the world's most popular social network (see Figure 4-2 for an example of a Facebook page).

Protocol

Social networking sites vary greatly based on their feature sets and raisons d'être, but there are some common elements across most of them. This section will introduce those elements.

Profiles

The building blocks of a social network are user pages, known as *profiles*. Your profile page can include information about you, including employment information, educational history, relationship status, contact information, and interests and hobbies. It can link to your photos and your friends' profiles, and allow visitors to contact you, often through private and public messaging. Social networking sites differ widely in how much they allow you to customize your profile: MySpace allows custom backgrounds and graphics, Facebook lets you add new blocks of content from applications, and LinkedIn gives you very little control. It's a good idea to do whatever you can to make your profile reflect your personality and personal brand, but don't go crazy—everyone hates the seizure-inducing profile with alarmingly loud pop music.

Profiles are for real people. You should have a profile; your company's logo should not. Profiles contain personal information; a brand can't have a favorite movie or book. If your company has a recognizable spokesperson, you can create a profile for him; otherwise, stick to a page or group for your company information.

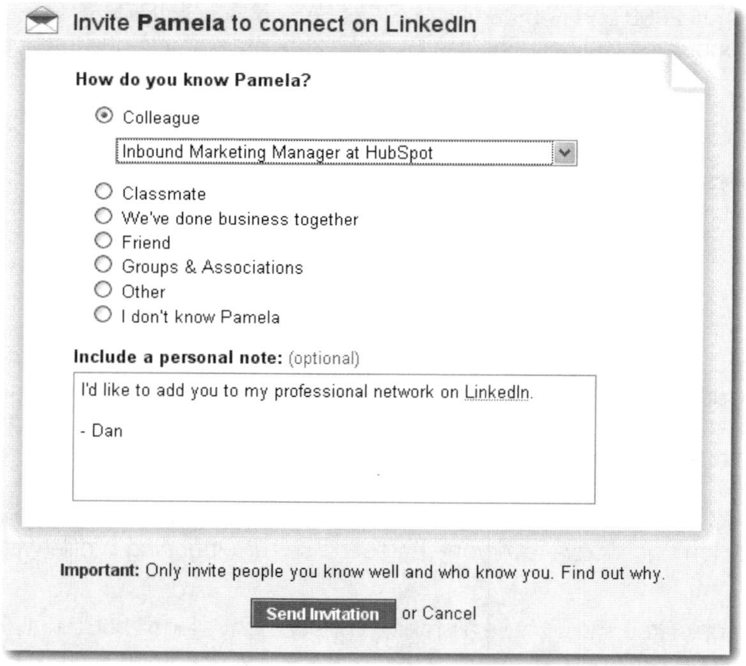

Invite **Pamela** to connect on LinkedIn

How do you know Pamela?

⊙ Colleague

Inbound Marketing Manager at HubSpot

○ Classmate
○ We've done business together
○ Friend
○ Groups & Associations
○ Other
○ I don't know Pamela

Include a personal note: (optional)

I'd like to add you to my professional network on LinkedIn.

- Dan

Important: Only invite people you know well and who know you. Find out why.

Send Invitation   or Cancel

Figure 4-3. This is an example of connecting with another user on LinkedIn.

Connecting

The most important action of a social network is the act of two people connecting. MySpace considers it *friending* regardless of the recipient, whereas Facebook reserves friending for individual people and calls it *fanning* when you connect with a brand. LinkedIn keeps it simple and calls everything *connecting* (see Figure 4-3).

Social networks were conceived to emphasize strong connections between people—the people you actually know in real life rather than your online buddies. Some users follow this maxim to the letter and will accept connection requests only from people they know well. Other users will connect with just about anyone. In either case, if you're sending a connection request to someone, and it isn't obvious how you know her, you should include a brief introductory sentence or two along with your request explaining why you should be friends.

Social networks impose limits on how many people you can connect to in a given amount of time. These restrictions are in place to thwart spammers trying to build giant networks; if you're running into warnings, you're probably doing something wrong and need to slow down. It's a building process, and there's no reason to go out and get a million friends in one day.

I once worked on a political campaign on Facebook, where we set up a profile for the candidate and began searching for people who were sympathetic to the candidate's causes to friend. After a burst of connecting to lots of potential supporters, the site would warn us that we were sending too many requests, and eventually the account was suspended. Although our account was reinstated after we sent a few emails to tech support, the exact limit was never revealed—all Facebook ever said was "too many."

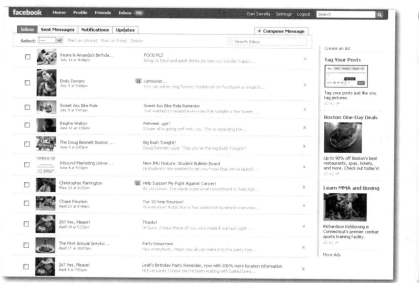
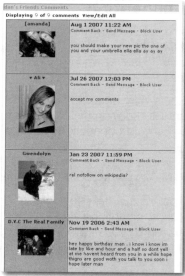

Figure 4-4. On the left is an example of a Facebook inbox; on the right, a MySpace inbox.

Private Messaging

Social networks all contain some form of private messaging akin to email (see Figure 4-4). These are typically sent from one user to another, but they can also be sent by a group to all of the group's friends. The networks will generally send the recipient an email notification of a received message, so don't bombard people's inboxes with constant message spam. If you find yourself wondering how to automatically send these messages, you're doing something wrong.

I've heard of someone being warned by Facebook for sending "too many" messages in a period of time. This person was actually conversing with his many friends.

Public Messaging

Public messages are called *comments* in MySpace and *wall messages* in Facebook. Commenting sections can be found on profiles, photos, groups, events, and business pages. When posting a public message, remember that everyone can read it. Don't share anything you wouldn't send to your boss and your mother. Congratulations, happy birthday, good luck, and long-time-no-see messages are all popular public messaging topics.

Marketers have been guilty of spamming the public message sections of related groups and pages—for example, while working for that politician I mentioned earlier, we were warned about "too many" wall posts. But don't be afraid to congratulate people on recent accomplishments.

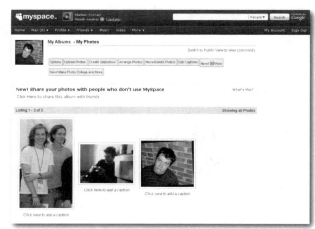

Figure 4-5. Here are examples of a Facebook group (left) and MySpace photos (right).

Groups

Most social networks contain the concept of a *group*—a collection of people joined by some common interest (see the lefthand side of Figure 4-5 for an example). Group members can share news and discussions, and the group's administrators can send private messages to everyone.

Nonmarketers create groups for a plethora of reasons, including the I-lost-my-cell-so-send-me-your-numbers group and the save-such-and-such-TV-show group. Starting and joining a group requires only a small amount of commitment in time and resources, and little to no member involvement; as a result, many people belong to tons of seemingly pointless groups. LinkedIn is the exception to this rule, as it displays the logos of the groups you're a member of on your profile, meaning that many users are more selective in deciding which groups to join.

Photos

One of the most popular features of social networking sites is the ability to share photos. In fact, Facebook's photo-sharing feature is more popular than all of the other photo-sharing sites on the Web combined. You can upload pictures of yourself and your friends, and tag people in the images with their names. Photos can also have their own comment sections, allowing you and your friends to talk about them.

Campaigns can be designed to encourage users to take photos that include your product and to post them to Facebook and MySpace (see the righthand side of Figure 4-5 for an example of MySpace photos).

Figure 4-6. One of the most popular applications on Facebook is the Causes application.

Events

Most social networks will allow you to create an event and invite your friends to attend it. These events most commonly occur in the real world, but some are online-only events. RSVP functionality is included, as are commenting and photo uploads.

Anytime you're hosting a local event, set up a social networking event page. Use it to invite all your business's fans to come and meet people from your company.

Applications

Social networks have exposed their functionality through application programming interfaces (APIs) to developers, allowing them to create applications that plug into their site. Some applications function as add-ons to a profile or page enhancing that functionality, whereas others work more like standalone applications inside the network that leverage the functionality contained in the site.

Some of the most popular applications extend existing social networking functionality by enhancing public messaging systems, adding calendars, or allowing you to indicate which connections you're related to. Other popular apps facilitate philanthropy (as shown in Figure 4-6), or allow you to play games such as Scrabble and poker with your friends.

Applications require technical resources and programming capabilities, but they can be worthwhile additions to a social media marketing campaign. The best apps will allow people to communicate and interact with their friends rather than just act as advertisements for a product.

Status Updates

Several social networking sites have begun to allow their users to post messages answering a simple question: "What are you doing?" The social networking equivalent of instant message (IM) away messages, *status updates* were originally just short text messages, but Facebook has begun to allow users to post images, links, and videos in their status updates as well. Status messages are often integrated with public messaging systems, allowing your friends to comment on your updates. Many people log in to social networks regularly just to read the status updates of their friends and stay up-to-date on their whereabouts and activities.

Privacy

Privacy is a sticky issue on social networks. Older users are generally more concerned about and aware of privacy. Younger users revel in sharing minute details of their lives with their entire social networks, and often need to be reminded that some content may be embarrassing or problematic later in life. If you're in marketing, you'll probably want to have open settings to connect with as many people as possible.

Keep in mind the age of your audience when planning a social media marketing campaign, and be sure not to ask for information that is more personal than your audience would feel comfortable providing. Also, carefully review the terms of service (ToS) of each social network before launching a campaign.

Facebook

Currently, Facebook is the dominant social networking site, and it has the most features useful to the social media marketer. It began in universities, so Facebook boasts a commanding percentage of college students as members. Recently, however, its fastest growing segment has been users older than 35, and recent data suggests that the 35–54 age group has become bigger than the 18–24 age group. For these older users, Facebook presents a middle ground between the stuffiness of LinkedIn and the adolescent playground of MySpace, and is a fun but easily navigable place where they can reconnect with old friends.

Pages

Facebook allows businesses to create public profiles that have many of the same features as a user's profile. Users can connect with a page and become fans. Pages can have public messaging walls, events, photos, and custom applications. Nearly every company engaged in social media marketing should have a Facebook page; it can often serve as a central place for the integration of other parts of a campaign.

One of the most popular pages on Facebook is the Coca-Cola page, yet it wasn't even created by the company itself. A Coke fan in Los Angeles made the page featuring little more than a giant can of soda, and in a few weeks it had 250,000 fans. At the time of this writing, it has more than 3.5 million fans. Facebook noticed the size of the group and asked Coca-Cola corporate to take it over, but the soda company's marketing team demonstrated its social media savvy and didn't charge in and strong-arm the original creator out of the picture. Instead, it assigned a team of people to help him maintain the page. If you go to that page today and post a comment such as "Pepsi is better than Coke," Coca-Cola corporate lets it stay. The best social media marketing is always going to be done by your fans, not by you, so get out of their way.

When you're setting up a page for your business, you can use a few applications to make the page more interesting to visitors and make them more likely to return.

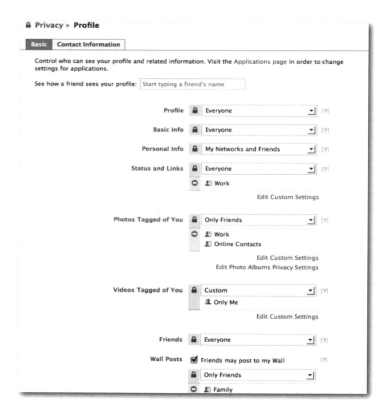

Figure 4-7. Facebook offers granular privacy settings.

Blog RSS Feed Reader (*http://www.facebook.com/apps/application.php?id=5315590686*)

> Your company should have a blog to keep customers and clients updated regarding product releases and other news. Make sure it has an RSS feed. Use this application to pull posts from your blog onto your Facebook page.

The Twitter App (*http://www.facebook.com/apps/application.php?id=2231777543*)

> Social media marketing often means your company has a Twitter account. Use the Twitter app to send your tweets to your Facebook page.

Static FBML (*http://www.facebook.com/apps/application.php?sid=59c8a2bba844922b5153efc9b9eba 237&id=4949752878&ref=s*)

> If you want to include special images or HTML on your page, you'll need to use the Static FBML app to accomplish that.

After you've integrated your existing content onto your Facebook page, it is important for you to include content that users can't get anywhere else. Avoid the urge to turn your page into a watered-down version of your website. Offer exclusive deals and content that are for Facebook fans only, or give your fans access to products before they are released elsewhere. This creates a sense of excitement for your fans.

Privacy Settings

Facebook features fine-grained settings that allow you to control the types of profile content that your friends will be able to see. The best way to use these settings is to divide your friends into lists, such as family members, coworkers, online buddies, and so on. In the Privacy section, you can then specify which groups can see which features (see Figure 4-7).

Figure 4-8. With the LinkedIn Introduction feature, a user can find a "path" of shared connections between herself and someone she wants to contact.

LinkedIn

The social networking site for business professionals, LinkedIn is the most restrictive social network in terms of customization and integration. It does not include any photo-sharing features, and was the last major social networking site to allow users to post photos of themselves to their profiles. The core function of LinkedIn is professional networking, so it is used heavily by job seekers and recruiters. LinkedIn restricts contact between members so that only individuals who are directly contacted can message each other. The LinkedIn features most useful to marketers are Groups and Answers.

LinkedIn is the only one of the three major social networking sites that charges a fee for some types of access. The paid-for features are focused on recruiters and allow them to post jobs and contact people they are not directly connected to.

Introductions

Because of the restrictions placed on messaging between users, LinkedIn has a feature called *Introductions*, where a user finds a "path" of shared connections between herself and someone she would like to contact. Each step along the way, she receives a request message, and can choose to not forward it or to continue the chain with a personalized message to one of her contacts (see Figure 4-8).

Introductions can be useful to the marketer who wants to find a personalized way to connect with a blogger or journalist through shared connections.

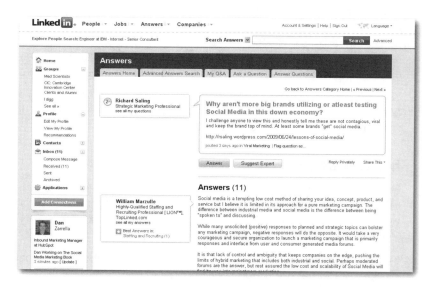

Figure 4-9. On the left is an example of the LinkedIn Recommendations feature; on the right is an example of the LinkedIn Answers feature.

Recommendations

A feature specific to LinkedIn is Recommendations. With this feature, users can write short endorsements of other users they've worked with in the past (see the lefthand side of Figure 4-9). During a job search, these recommendations can function as a form of reference.

Answers

Nonpaying LinkedIn users can also post up to 10 questions per month that will be answered by the community. Answering questions is an easy technique for marketers who wish to establish thought leadership and name recognition in a specific field. You can subscribe to the RSS feed for specific categories of questions to be alerted when a new question is added. Questions are open to answers for one week, and there is an advantage to being the first to answer—you should check for new questions often.

Answers can be marked as "good" or "best," which awards the answerer points. If your answer is flagged as a best answer, your profile is labeled as that of an expert. Questioners prefer in-depth responses that provide detailed and specific information, and that don't include pitches for commercial products or services. Remember, you're trying to establish yourself as a thought leader, not peddle your wares. The righthand side of Figure 4-9 shows an example of the LinkedIn Answers feature.

MySpace

MySpace was the first social networking site to allow users to customize their profiles. It maintains popularity with teens, musicians, and other artists. It still gives the user more freedom to customize than any of the other networks, and many users have abused this ability with heaps of blinking graphics and music that plays automatically. For marketers interested in reaching urban, nightlife, or music communities, MySpace is a good choice. Outside of that, however, its use is limited in comparison to Facebook and LinkedIn.

Figure 4-10. Rapper Jay-Z has a highly customized MySpace profile.

Blogs

MySpace has an easy-to-use blogging feature linked from user profiles. Once you've set up a MySpace profile, you can easily start to write a blog inside the network. The marketing tactics I mentioned in Chapter 2 also apply to blogging on MySpace. You can subscribe to these blogs to be updated on new posts.

Bulletins

A *bulletin* is like a public message that goes to all of your friends on MySpace. Be aware that everyone will see these, and that people dislike being bombarded over and over again with posts—this is like receiving email spam. You can use bulletins to announce upcoming promotional dates, or to ask for feedback on new pieces of content you've added to your profile, but don't do this more than once or twice a week.

MySpace for Musicians

Bands and music artists should sign up for artist profiles on MySpace (for an example, see Figure 4-10). One of the most important features is being allowed to post a number of songs on your band's site. This is critical to give people access to your music so that they can see whether they like it. Add some photos of the band and customize the profile to match your brand image, but don't fall into common usability traps: go easy on the animated graphics, and ensure that your text color is readable against your background color.

Search for and add your fans as friends. When they add you, head over to their profiles. It is common to post to a profile and thank the person in the comment section for adding you. Much like the standard "If you like this, you'll love this" recommendation system, send friend requests to the people listed in profiles of bands similar to yours. Once you've started to build an audience, you can use the blogging and bulletin features to let everyone know about upcoming shows and releases.

Takeaway Tips

- Social networks allow you to build direct and personal relationships with your customers.

- People should have profiles; companies should have pages.

- Set-it-and-forget-it is not a good social network marketing strategy. Be active with updates and interaction.

- Know your audience and select the social networks where they can be found.

- Understand the special features offered by social networks and use them.

- Don't excessively use public or private messaging systems (spam)—use them only for the good stuff.

- Motivate your fans to create content on social networking sites for you. Organic content is much more convincing.

- Give your fans a place to interact with your company and one another.

- Offer content that is exclusive to social networks, and don't just rebuild your website.

CHAPTER 5

Media Sharing

Introduction

Media-sharing sites allow users to create and upload multimedia content, sometimes called user-generated content (UGC). With the advent of easy-to-use digital cameras and camcorders as well as high-speed Internet connections, media-sharing sites have become extremely popular. Marketers can create videos with very little expertise and upload them to YouTube to reach millions of users.

Although these sites include social features for members, most of the users of media-sharing sites are not members, but are merely viewing the sites' content. When you create content for use in your blog, upload the content to a sharing site to allow others to use it as well.

Figure 5-1. IFILM was one of the first social media–sharing sites.

Figure 5-2. Tags are used on a variety of sites, and come in many forms.

History

One of the earliest media-sharing sites, IFILM.net, was launched in 1997 as an online collection of short videos where users could also submit their own work (see Figure 5-1). Back then, video was streamed using browser plug-ins such as Windows Media Player, QuickTime, and RealPlayer, and most people had dial-up connections, which made watching videos a very slow process.

In 2002, Flash MX was released, and the web video we know today was made possible. Now you no longer needed to download a special streaming video player; MX introduced the ability to include and play videos within a Flash file. Sites such as YouTube, which was launched in 2005, were suddenly possible.

In 1999, three photo-sharing communities were born. Ofoto, Shutterfly, and Webshots allowed users to upload their pictures and share them with the world. Before these sites (and even after them), you had to use a host such as Geocities or Angelfire to upload your photos to your home page via FTP.

Spawned by the rise in popularity of MySpace, photo-sharing sites such as Photobucket and ImageShack were launched in 2003 with the idea that people should be able to upload their images there and then display them on their profiles. Social media sharing didn't really hit its stride until 2004, when Flickr was launched, combining easy photo uploading with tagging and social networking functionality (see Figure 5-2 for examples of tags).

Protocol

Social media–sharing sites allow users to share a wide range of media types, but many features are present on all of them. This section will detail some of those features.

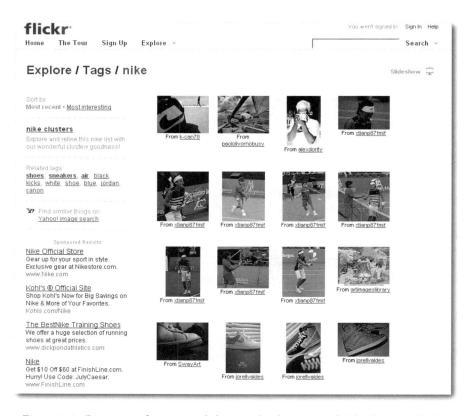

Figure 5-3. Consumers have posted thousands of pictures of Nike shoes to Flickr.

Tags

A *tag* is a word assigned to a piece of content that helps describe it (e.g., *book, work, blog, social media*). A single piece of media can be tagged with multiple words, and tags are used to search content that is not textual, such as videos and photos; for instance, Figure 5-3 shows examples of media tagged with *Nike*. Tags are nonhierarchical, meaning they are not organized into a parent-child tree structure, and they are created by users rather than being determined by the site owner. The first use of a tag "creates" the category that all content with that tag falls into.

Social media sites typically support one of two types of tags: space separated and comma separated. Space-separated tags are entered in a list with a space between the tags. In space-separated tags, you can't have a single tag with a space inside it; if you wanted a tag called "social media" you would write it as "socialmedia." Some sites allow spaces if you enclose the tag in quotes. Comma-separated tags are written as a list with commas between the tags, so you can use spaces inside the tags.

It's a good idea to err on the side of too many tags, rather than too few—when in doubt, add more tags. Think of them like a pyramid; start with the most specific words, such as the name of the person or place in the photo or video, and don't forget the little things people can see: is there a cool car in the background? Then move on to more categorical words: is it an ocean landscape or a sports blooper? Tags are how your content will be found in a search, so try to think of every relevant word someone might search for.

Digital Asset Optimization

Your company likely produces lots of content already: PowerPoint slideshows, graphs, and maybe even webinars and videos. *Digital asset optimization* (DAO) is the process of taking stock of the digital content you already have and getting it online and into social media where it can help drive buzz and traffic. With the introduction of universal and blended search—where multimedia content is displayed in regular

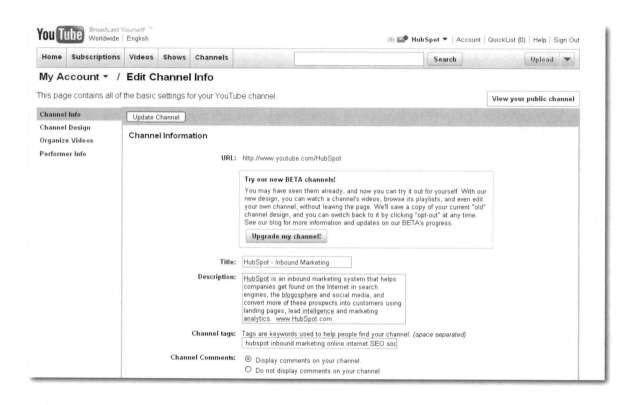

Figure 5-4. YouTube allows you to customize your channel.

search engine results—many traditional search engine marketers have begun to tout DAO as the "easy" way into social media.

However, you should not view DAO as an alternative to creating new content. Content must be engaging and unique to resonate with viewers. Simply reusing your old slide decks won't help you "go viral."

Organic Content

There are essentially two ways in which content is posted to media-sharing sites, such as YouTube, SlideShare, Flickr, or a blog, that you should be interested in. The first is when a company creates and publishes content; the second is when people outside the company organically create media about the content. The former type is important, especially in the early stages of using social marketing for your company, but the latter is the Holy Grail of social marketing. Whenever possible, encourage your fans to remix the media you have posted or to create their own content about your company.

YouTube

Started in 2005 by three PayPal employees, and funded to the tune of $11.5 million by the respected venture capital fund Sequoia Capital, YouTube is currently the largest video-sharing site on the Web and the third most visited site on the Internet. It has changed the face of the Web, and there is hardly a marketing campaign that would not find value in a presence on YouTube.

Your Profile

User accounts on YouTube are called *channels*. When creating an account on YouTube, you can customize your channel in various ways (see Figure 5-4). The first and most important step in creating your

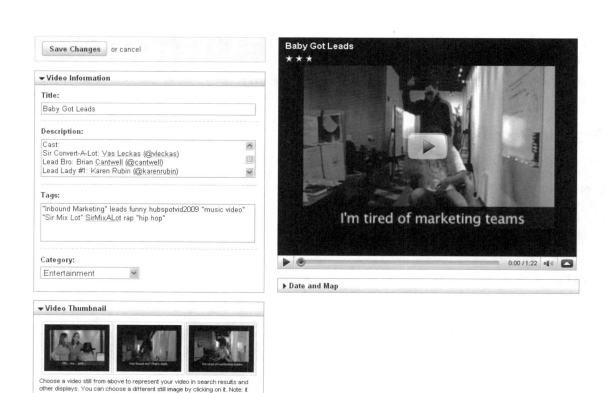

Figure 5-5. YouTube provides an interface that allows you to edit the details of your videos.

account is choosing a username; you cannot change your username, and your username will determine your YouTube URL. This custom URL is invaluable to directing customers to your YouTube channel. If you're setting up a channel for your business, use your business name; if it's a personal account, use your real name. If these aren't available, pick something that you'll be happy with in five years. Choose a name that is short, pronounceable, and unique.

The title of your channel's page is also customizable, and should be either a business name or a personal name, or some keywords that define what your videos are about. Your profile's Description field is a great place to introduce yourself to your audience and include contact information, such as a website or email address. The tags you choose should include the various words that people could use to search for you or your content.

YouTube also allows you to customize your profile with specific foreground and background colors as well as fonts, and you can hide or rearrange specific parts of your profile. Use these features to echo your existing brand colors, but be careful to make sure your page is still readable: dark text on a dark background can be hard to read and may deter visitors.

Your Videos

Watching a video online is a large commitment of attention; unlike other forms of media consumption, it is nearly impossible to multitask while browsing YouTube. Because of this, when it comes to videos, shorter is better. In addition, your videos must be very engaging. People will not sit for 10 minutes watching your CFO in front of a plain white background drone on about TPS reports. You must strive to keep your audience engaged the entire time they're watching your videos. Figure 5-5 shows an example of the options that are available to you when you upload a video.

Honors for this video (20)

#6 - Most Discussed (This Month) - India
#2 - Most Discussed (This Month) - Entertainment - India
#1 - Most Responded (Today) - India
#1 - Most Responded (Today) - Entertainment - India
#31 - Most Responded (Today) - Entertainment
#1 - Most Responded (This Week) - India
#1 - Most Responded (This Week) - Entertainment - India
#29 - Most Responded (This Week) - Entertainment
#1 - Most Responded (This Month) - India
#1 - Most Responded (This Month) - Entertainment - India
#100 - Most Responded (This Month) - Entertainment
#10 - Most Responded (All Time) - India
#2 - Most Responded (All Time) - Entertainment - India
#4 - Most Viewed (This Month) - India
#2 - Most Viewed (This Month) - Entertainment - India
#84 - Most Viewed (This Month) - Entertainment
#13 - Top Favorited (This Month) - India
#5 - Top Favorited (This Month) - Entertainment - India
#14 - Top Rated (This Month) - India
#5 - Top Rated (This Month) - Entertainment - India

Figure 5-6. YouTube's honors categories list the honors a video has received.

Like most social media users, YouTubers are very sensitive to product pitches, so keep your contributions as noncommercial as you can. If your commercial content is extremely entertaining or informational, it may be tolerated, but this is the exception, not the rule. You should be including calls to action in your videos, but you'll need to be very creative about them.

For example, my company often puts a trailer at the end of a video showing a user searching for *inbound marketing*, but no mention of the company's name. However, that search will return *HubSpot* within the top 10 results.

When uploading videos, you'll be given the option to allow people to embed your video. Embedding lets anyone copy a line of HTML code from YouTube and then paste it to his site, which then displays it there, like in a blog post. Here is an example of the code that users can use to embed your videos on their sites:

```
<object width="560" height="340"><param name="movie" value="http://www.youtube.com/v/
llJVQODwlqo&hl=en&fs=1&"></param>

<param name="allowFullScreen" value="true"></param><param name="allowscriptaccess"
value="always"></param><embed

src="http://www.youtube.com/v/llJVQODwlqo&hl=en&fs=1&" type="application/x-shockwave-flash"
allowscriptaccess="always"

allowfullscreen="true" width="560" height="340"></embed></object>
```

This is the kind of viral content sharing that you should be striving for—you want people to spread the word for you. So, for videos, you should not only allow embedding, but actively encourage it.

YouTube has an "honors" section that lists the most actively watched videos in each category. For example, there are category lists for the most viewed, commented, favorited, rated, and responded-to videos (see Figure 5-6). These lists are generated by an algorithm that measures activity over time,

Figure 5-7. Flickr's home page is streamlined and easy to follow.

which can drive lots of views to your videos. When you first upload your video, start promoting it right away—your goal is to get it on one of these honors lists. Post it to your blog and Facebook page, tweet about it, and send it out in an email newsletter.

YouTube users see automatically generated thumbnail images of each video. You, as the video owner, are shown three different thumbnails to choose from. The thumbnail is the first exposure a user will have to your video, so it is very important to make it as enticing as possible.

Flickr

Flickr is the modern king of photo-sharing sites (even though Facebook photos are used more, this service does not make them publicly viewable). Flickr is a great place to execute digital asset optimization by uploading graphs and charts as well as photos of your work (see Figure 5-7). For example, if you work for a clothing brand, post photos of models wearing your latest designs.

Tara Kirchner of the Flickr marketing team advises that the first step a marketer should take before using Flickr is to read the community guidelines, because the Flickr community can "have teeth" when dealing with corporate content; in other words, if they sense an overly commercial bent to your content, they'll react strongly. Tara also pointed out that Flickr is best used to tell your company's story, rather than simply conduct advertising. For example, a candy company could post photos of a factory tour, and a baseball team could show off historical photos.

Remember, when you upload photos, you are contributing to the Web's largest publicly accessible photo archive—what unique images does your company have that you can give to the community? Flickr is not a good place to put head shots of the board of directors, so you should really think about your strategy before posting images.

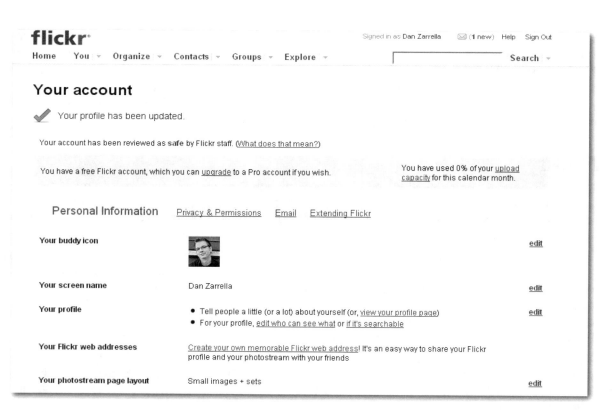

Figure 5-8. You can edit your personal information on Flickr.

Tara also recommended an internally focused approach: for instance, a few employees set up personal accounts, add images about the company, and tag them with the company name, rather than create one "branded" company account. This creates a more personal outreach.

Your Profile

As on YouTube, your profile is of utmost importance on Flickr. You can change your username on Flickr, so try experimenting with different combinations to see what works best for you: your full name, your company name, or your site's URL. The next step is to choose a Flickr URL; you cannot change this, so make it count. Your name is the best choice. Add a little bit of text about yourself or your company in the description, including a few links to your site (see Figure 5-8).

Flickr has two types of accounts: free and paid. Paid accounts aren't very expensive and give you more storage space for photos and a little "pro" icon next to your username, which can do wonders for your credibility. Paid accounts will also give you access to information about how people are finding your account.

Your Photos

When you upload a photo, you'll have options for a title, description, and tags (see Figure 5-9). The photo title will become the title of that image's page, so pay special attention to this and include some keywords. The Description field allows HTML, so include links to your site and a brief description of what users are looking at.

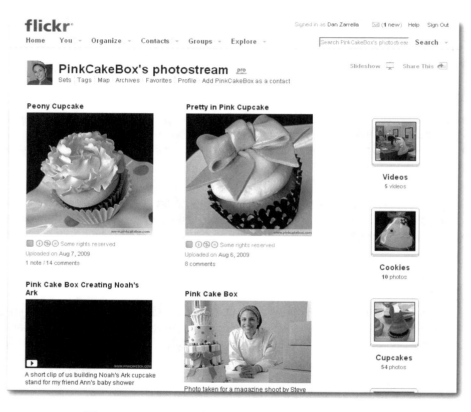

Figure 5-9. Here is a delicious example of Flickr photos.

If you're uploading a bunch of related images, put them in a set. Collecting similar images into sets makes it easier for viewers who've liked one of your photos to find more they'll like. If you're a paid user—which you should be—you can also aggregate related sets into collections; this becomes useful if you have a lot of images.

Creative Commons

Creative Commons is a set of copyright licenses designed to make it easy for content creators and content users to understand open licensing. You select from one of four conditions that determine how your content can be reused:

Attribution
> Reuses must credit the original author.

NoDerivs
> The content may not be remixed and distributed.

NonCommercial
> The content may not be used for commercial purposes.

ShareAlike
> Subsequent versions of the content must be released under a compatible licensing scheme.

Flickr makes it easy for users to mark their work with a Creative Commons license. Take advantage of this: use one of these open licenses to encourage people to use and share your photos.

Figure 5-10. A tag page on Flickr is a great way to showcase all the content that has been created around your brand.

Other Features

Flickr is a social site; don't forget its community features. Search for groups related to your company, join them, and share your photos with the groups. But don't spam groups, and share only the images that are interesting and relevant. You should also check out other users' pictures, comment on the ones you like, and favorite the ones you really like.

When you're encouraging your fans to make media for you, ask them to use a special, unique tag when they upload images to Flickr. You can then link to a page on Flickr that will show every image from that campaign. This is a great way to showcase all the awesome organic content that has been created around your brand (see Figure 5-10).

Flickr also has a slideshow feature that allows you to put a group of photos into an interactive block that users can scroll through. You can make a slideshow out of sets, tag pages, or search results. They make great additions to blog posts, too.

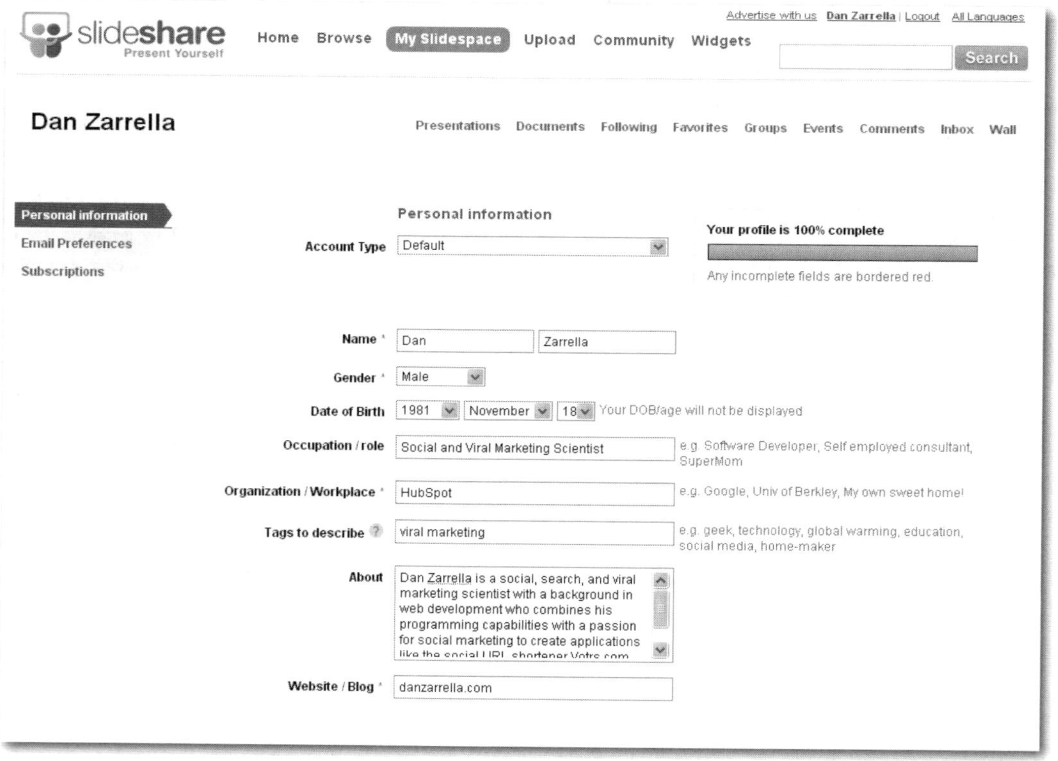

Figure 5-11. The registration form on SlideShare asks you to provide information about yourself.

SlideShare

SlideShare is a media-sharing site that allows you to upload and share presentations. The presentations are turned into YouTube-style Flash widgets that can be embedded on other sites and blogs—which you should encourage your visitors to do.

Your Profile

When you sign up for an account at SlideShare, you'll be given a choice to select the type of account you'd like to create. The *company account* option gives you space to enter the size and industry of your company, and the *professional speaker* type allows you to enter three conferences you've spoken at as well as links to your talks. The *default* type is best for individuals who do not fit into either of the preceding categories.

The registration form will ask you for information, including your title, workplace, some details about yourself, and a link to your site or blog (see Figure 5-11). Take some time when providing this information to personalize your account. SlideShare also allows you to upload a photograph of yourself, which you should do as well; use the same photo you're using on other sites to reinforce your brand image.

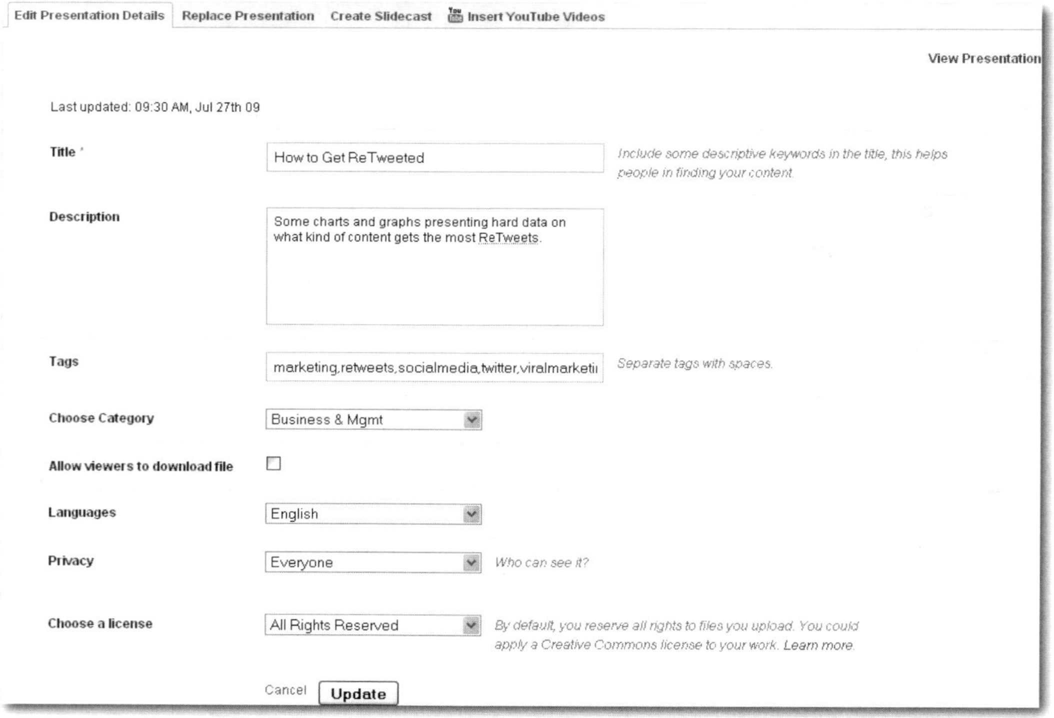

Figure 5-12. You are asked to provide a variety of details regarding your presentation, including a brief description.

Your Presentations

As with YouTube, watching a presentation is an attention-consuming task, so don't waste your viewers' time. Keep slideshows as short as possible while still including valuable information—that means no filler slides. And remember that the SlideShare widget is only a few hundred pixels in size, so keep the fonts on your slides large enough to be legible. Pay special attention to this when constructing your title slide, because the first slide becomes the presentation's thumbnail when it appears in other places. Your first slide must be easy to read and enticing enough to persuade the browser to stop and check it out.

When you upload your presentation, pick a good title for it, as this will become the URL your viewers will use to find your slides. Keep the title short and include keywords. Provide a brief summary of your presentation in the Description field, and keep the most important information at the beginning, since the site will display only the first few lines of the description, unless the user clicks a "More" link. SlideShare also provides a list of tags you can use to label your video. Figure 5-12 shows the details you are asked to provide regarding your SlideShare presentation.

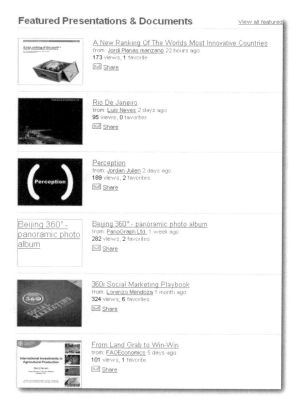

Figure 5-13. SlideShare showcases popular presentations and documents on its home page.

Other Features

SlideShare has a list of "featured" presentations on its home page (see Figure 5-13) that are determined by an algorithm that works similar to the YouTube honors lists: measuring activity over time. If you'd like have your presentation appear here (and you should; it can drive a ton of views), you should focus on sending a lot of people to your presentation as soon as you upload it. A good way to do this is to upload your slides the day before you present them at a conference and tell the audience during your talk that they can get the slides on SlideShare.

SlideShare recently added functionality that allows you to include a YouTube video in your presentation. This is a simple way to link your social media–sharing efforts. And don't forget that SlideShare is a social site, so go and make friends. Find groups that will be interested in your presentations, join them, and share your slides. Find other presentations that you like, comment on them, and favorite them.

Takeaway Tips

- Media-sharing sites make it easy for you to produce and distribute multimedia content to thousands or millions of viewers.

- Leverage all your existing media by posting it to media-sharing sites.

- Use tags effectively; always include more than you think you need.

- Shorter is better when it comes to videos; produce bite-size content.

- Use open licensing and embedding features to encourage your viewers to share your media for you.

- Inspire your fans to create organic content about your brand.

CHAPTER 6

Social News and Bookmarking

Introduction

Social news sites are websites that allow users to submit and vote on content from around the Web. This voting activity helps isolate the most interesting links. Marketers have found these sites to be very useful for generating buzz and traffic around specific campaigns or articles, but direct marketing on social news sites is typically frowned upon.

Social bookmarking sites are similar to social news sites, but the value presented to users is focused on allowing them to collect and store interesting links they've found and may wish to revisit. Most bookmarking sites count the number of times a piece of content has been stored and interpret these as votes to highlight the most valuable links (see Figure 6-1).

History

The first social bookmarking site, ITList, launched in April 1996, and from that point until the pop of the first dot-com bubble, a plethora of sites offering public and private online storage of your favorite links emerged. However, most of them died in the late 1990s.

In 1997, Slashdot was launched as a place where users could submit links to technology stories. It became enormously popular, and was the first social media site to wield server-crushing amounts of traffic, known as the *Slashdot Effect*, when a link was posted to its home page. Two years later, a site called Fark was launched to serve a less technical and more irreverent niche. Shortly after its launch, Fark expanded to allow readers other than the site's owner to upload links.

Figure 6-1. Sphinn is an example of the numerous niche social voting sites on the Web.

Social news and bookmarking reached its widest audience with the advent of Delicious in 2003 and Digg in 2004. Digg relies on the wisdom of its audience to filter the most interesting articles from the thousands that are submitted every day.

Protocol

Social news sites focus on delivering the latest news based on votes. Bookmarking sites allow users to save links for later reading; the number of saves counts as votes and the most popular links are displayed. These sites all have certain elements that are useful to marketers. This section will introduce you to those elements.

Your Profile

Social news and bookmarking sites each have slight variations regarding user profiles. For those that allow you to upload an avatar image (and most do), you should use the same image across all sites; this should also be consistent across social networks and any other sites where you have a profile. Fill out as much profile information as you can, including instant messenger (IM) names, profiles on other sites, and links to your websites. Some sites also allow you to friend other users, as on social networks; find people submitting and voting on content similar to yours and connect with them.

The more active and consistent you are in contributing to a site, the more valuable your account will become; you'll begin to develop a reputation, and other people will be more receptive to your stories. If you are a regular reader of blogs and news sources in your niche, you'll have the advantage of being the first person to submit major stories.

Figure 6-2. Most social news sites feature embeddable voting badges.

Submitting

To get your content listed on a social news site, you have to submit it. During the submission process, you'll be asked to provide a headline, a short description of the content of the page, the category it should be listed in, and some tags to describe it.

Most communities frown on people who submit their own content, so avoid doing this. Instead, cultivate a community of active social news users on your site, and display links for them to submit your content. Making friends with power users is also a great idea, and it's something I'll talk about a little later in this chapter.

Voting

The central action of interest to marketers on social news sites is voting. Different sites call it different things, and some don't even specifically label it, but the idea is the same: a piece of content is submitted to a site, and other users vote on it, either up or down. The number, quality, and speed of votes determine how popular your content is. Pieces of content that receive sufficient votes are promoted to a section of popular content, a process called *going pop* that I'll detail later in this chapter.

Many social news sites offer badges that you can copy and paste onto your site (see Figure 6-2). Once your content has been submitted to one of these bookmarking sites, add a badge to your page so that your readers can vote it up or down without leaving your site. These buttons are great for promoting your content. You should place them as prominently on your content as you can when you think that a specific page has a good chance of doing well on a certain social site.

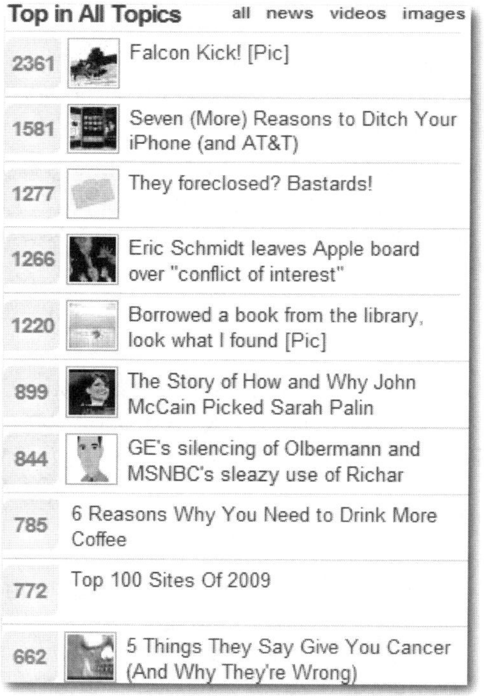

Top in All Topics all news videos images

2361		Falcon Kick! [Pic]
1581		Seven (More) Reasons to Ditch Your iPhone (and AT&T)
1277		They foreclosed? Bastards!
1266		Eric Schmidt leaves Apple board over "conflict of interest"
1220		Borrowed a book from the library, look what I found [Pic]
899		The Story of How and Why John McCain Picked Sarah Palin
844		GE's silencing of Olbermann and MSNBC's sleazy use of Richar
785		6 Reasons Why You Need to Drink More Coffee
772		Top 100 Sites Of 2009
662		5 Things They Say Give You Cancer (And Why They're Wrong)

Figure 6-3. In many instances, the headline of an article is the only thing a reader will see.

Headlines

On a social voting site, the most important element of a story is the headline. This has the greatest effect on how many votes a story gets, and is the only thing many users will read. The title of a blog post or a page is typically what a user submits, so spend some time writing a great headline (see Figure 6-3).

Good headlines give the impression that the content that follows them is easy to digest, entertaining, and valuable. Try to explain exactly what the user will get out of reading your content. If your content is a photo or a video, specify that in the title; if it is a list (such as a top 10 best list), put that in the headline.

Your titles should be eye-catching and provocative, but not misleading. Users on social sites are very savvy and will figure out your tricks much faster than you think.

Linkerati

Coined by Rand Fishkin of SEOmoz, the term *linkerati* refers to a class of individuals on the Web who are more likely than other users to have their own blogs or websites where they can link to content they find interesting. When marketing to social news sites, the linkerati are your target, as many of them frequent these sites and will blog about content they find there. Research I did on Digg in 2007 showed that the average popular page got about 300 links.

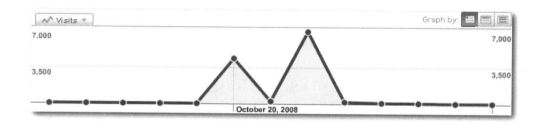

Figure 6-4. Going popular on a social news site will drive a large but temporary spike in traffic.

Going Pop

The ultimate goal of marketing on social news sites is to get your content listed as "popular." Voting sites have sections, typically on their home page, where they display the content that has been voted as most popular. Once a page has enough votes and is exposed to a larger audience, it will often start an avalanche of increasing vote counts; stories that have gone popular often have many more votes than those that have not (see Figure 6-4). Appearing here can drive tens of thousands of visits to your site and get it in front of the linkerati; the combination of these two actions often results in hundreds or thousands of incoming links.

The Digg Effect

When your content is listed on the front page of a site such as Digg (especially during peak daytime hours), your server will be hit with a crush of visitors, sometimes thousands per minute. Most shared-hosting environments have trouble dealing with traffic volumes this large, and having an unresponsive page squanders most of the benefit of going popular. You can solve this problem by either upgrading your server or implementing a caching system. The goal of a caching system is to ensure that your pages are not requesting information from a database on every page load, which is often what causes a site to crash during periods of high activity. Talk to your technical person to figure out the best solution before you start submitting pages to social news sites.

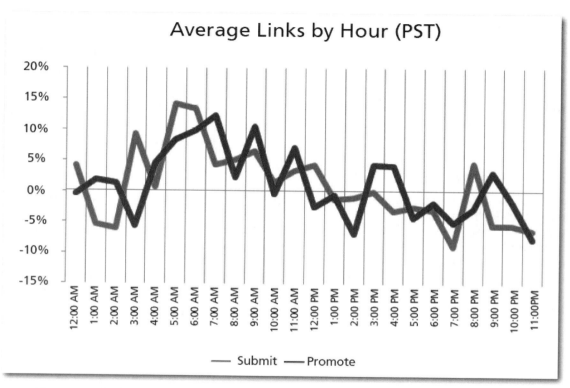

Figure 6-5. *The best time to submit your content is 22 hours before you want it to go popular, typically early in the morning.*

Timing

The number of people who vote on your content—and see it once it goes popular—is largely a function of timing. Hitting the front page of a social news site in the middle of the night will not result in the kind of traffic spike that comes from going popular during business hours. Many sites have a window of time from submission during which a site can go popular; stories on Digg, for instance, have 24 hours to make the front page. Getting a story submitted on Digg 18 to 22 hours before a peak usage hour is ideal, meaning you should be looking for submissions between 4:00 a.m. and midnight (see Figure 6-5).

Power Users

Certain users gain recognition and authority on the basis of the quality, consistency, and longevity of their submissions. This type of power user often has hundreds of friends who will vote for almost every story he submits; this means the content he posts is more likely to become popular than content posted by an unknown user.

One strategy for promoting your content is befriending these power users. Digg allows users to display their IM usernames, so you can find users who appear on the front page often and seem to enjoy content related to yours, and then say hi to them via IM. Be cautious when approaching these users, and don't start pitching your content at them right away; get to know them and the content they like, follow them on Twitter, and build relationships before you start asking for favors.

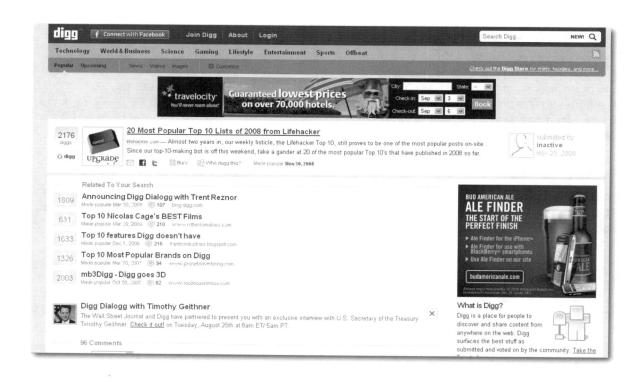

Figure 6-6. As with many other types of social media, social news sites love lists.

Reciprocity

The concept of "you scratch my back, I'll vote on your stories" is a controversial but powerful one. When you make friends on social news sites, the common understanding is that this friendship is built on sharing and voting on one another's stories. Some users compile lists of their voting buddies' IM names or email addresses and share stories with them that way. This activity borders on violating most news sites' terms of service (ToS), so as a new user, you shouldn't do it.

Content Types

A number of content formats typically work well on social voting sites:

Lists

> Top 10 types of lists give off the scent of easy-to-read content, and people love to rank things. Write a list of the 10 best, the 7 worst, the 9 geekiest, or the 5 most expensive things in your industry (see Figure 6-6).

Breaking news

> When big news breaks, it appears in the popular lists on most voting sites quickly. If you can be the first to write about something big happening, you'll have a good shot at going popular.

Games

> Casual games that can be played in a browser window do well on these types of sites. Simple, addictive games can be developed with minimal investment by most coders.

Figure 6-7. Digg is the most popular social news and voting site.

Controversy

Social media users love to argue; if you can present a well-constructed argument against a commonly held belief, you can get lots of votes. This works well when used against corporations, groups, or people perceived as "bad." The RIAA and Microsoft are favorite targets.

Videos and photos

Short videos and surprising photographs (especially in collections) are easy and quick for viewers to consume, and are well received by social news and voting sites.

Digg

Digg (see Figure 6-7) is the most popular social news site and the standard by which all others are measured. It is the most well-known site of its kind, and although it has made great strides to include non-geeky news, its core users are now and always have been twentysomething male techies. When a story reaches the Digg front page, it appears at the top of a chronological list and is pushed farther down the page as newer stories are promoted. Because Digg is so active, a story will appear on the front page for only a few hours.

Digg's negative voting comes in the form of *buries*. The number of negative votes is not shown, and the exact weight of a down vote compared to an up vote is unknown. The site is home to a boogeyman of sorts in the mythical "bury brigade," a supposedly organized group of users who bury any stories they don't like. Common targets are those that support organizations or topics disliked by the community, such as Microsoft or marketing.

Figure 6-8. Submitting a link to Digg is fast and easy.

If your content is not standard geek fare, you can still get on the front page of Digg by spinning your content with a technical angle. If your business is house painting, you can write an article about the 10 best ways to paint the Digg logo on the side of a building; if you sell furniture, try collecting pictures of geeky office fixtures. Be cautious with this tactic, as this audience is quite savvy and has learned to recognize obvious front-page attempts. But try out a few new types of content to expand your reach and see what works for you.

Once you submit a link to Digg (see Figure 6-8), it has 24 hours to reach the front page. The algorithm controlling promotion is shrouded in mystery, but it is probably composed of factors including the number and speed of votes, the variety of users voting, the number of comments left on a story, and a measurement of trust associated with a domain. Most of the articles that do well on Digg are from popular news sites and blogs; one way around this is to place your content on a trusted domain and promote that URL. For instance, you could create a video, upload it to YouTube, and get the YouTube link submitted as opposed to your own, relatively unknown domain.

Digg has a strong tradition of power users and a robust networking component, which makes the submitter of an article very important. Some articles will go popular after 80 votes, and some won't despite getting well more than 200 votes. Stories that don't reach Digg's front page receive very little traffic, but those that do can expect tens of thousands of hits in a few hours.

Going popular on Digg can result in hundreds of links, so it has become a target for many marketers. Because of this, it has sophisticated algorithms in place to thwart gaming, and it has become increasingly difficult to get pieces of content from domains that aren't very well known onto its front page.

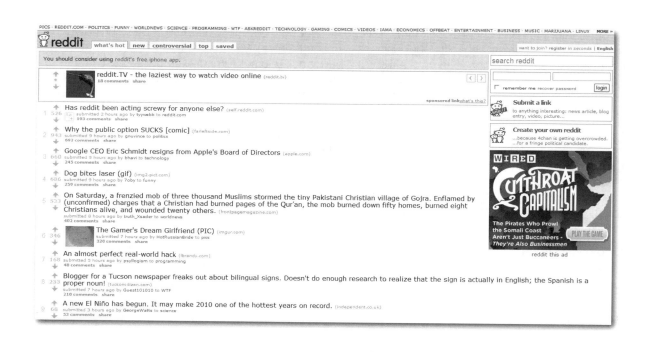

Figure 6-9. Reddit is another popular social news site.

Reddit

Perennially in second place in the social voting race, Reddit still drives substantial amounts of traffic (see Figure 6-9). And, as opposed to the all-or-nothing nature of Digg, Reddit sends some traffic to stories that don't quite go pop. Reddit's front page works more like a leader board than Digg's chronological list system. Stories can move up or down on it as they are voted on, meaning that a story can stay in a prominent position on Reddit for longer than it can on Digg.

Reddit has very little social networking functionality, so the power accounts aren't as important on Reddit as they are on other sites. Redditors are similar to Diggers (twentysomething geeks), albeit the former are slightly more educated and gender neutral.

Down-voting on Reddit is done by way of a down arrow that is placed directly under the corresponding up arrow. A story's score is the number of positive votes it has received minus the number of negative votes, and both numbers are displayed clearly, making Reddit the most transparent site in this regard. Content that gets a lot of up and down votes can appear on a separate "controversial" section of the site, meaning that a few down votes isn't the worst thing that can happen.

Figure 6-10. Here is a typical example of a popular story on Reddit.

Reddit seems to place a lot of weight on the speed of voting; stories that get tens of votes in the first hour can get to the bottom of Reddit's front page. If some of your content gets submitted, you should act quickly and add a voting badge to it to encourage a speedy influx of votes. Figure 6-10 shows an example of a popular story on Reddit.

Reddit is composed of multiple *sub-Reddits* for different categories. Users can select which sections they see on the home page, so category selection is crucial. When a user visits the Reddit home page, she will see popular stories from a handful of default sections, including Comics, Funny, Pics, Politics, Programming, Science, Technology, World News, WTF, and a miscellaneous "Reddit.com" sub-Reddit. These sections get much more traffic than the others, so focus on them when submitting.

Figure 6-11. StumbleUpon has more mainstream appeal than Digg.

StumbleUpon

Perhaps the most mainstream social bookmarking site, StumbleUpon also differs from the standard voting site interface. Rather than a front page with a list of popular links, StumbleUpon lets users interact with it through a browser plug-in that allows them to "stumble" from page to page across the Web with the click of a button. When you see a page you like anywhere on the Internet, you click on a thumbs-up icon—as opposed to the thumbs-down icon for bad content. The system learns what kinds of content you like from these votes and starts to show you targeted pages as you stumble.

Most social news sites send a huge spike of traffic in the hours after a story goes popular, that tapers off quickly. StumbleUpon, however, has been known to send wave after wave of traffic to pages that were first discovered (*submitted* in StumbleUpon lingo) months ago. It also exhibits less all-or-nothing behavior, as a few votes can result in a couple of thousand hits.

Because of its older, less technical audience, StumbleUpon favors less geeky content, impressive photographs, short videos, and games (see Figure 6-11). The personalization system also allows a wider range of topics to be delivered to interested audiences. If you're having trouble giving your story a nerdy enough angle to do well on Digg, StumbleUpon might be the right place for you.

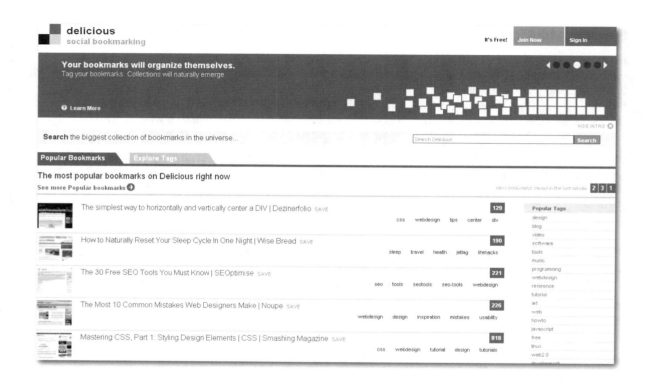

Figure 6-12. Delicious is a pure bookmarking site compared to Digg's social news and voting angle.

Delicious

Delicious focuses on storing your bookmarked links, and its social functionality takes a bit of a back seat. Bookmarking a page counts as a vote, and there is no down-voting mechanism. Stories that are saved enough times in a day or two (the exact threshold varies, but it is a bit more than 100) are shown on the Delicious front page and get a few thousand hits (see Figure 6-12).

From the user's perspective, bookmarking is a different action than voting, so the short-form content that does well on other social news sites doesn't work as well on Delicious. Users are more likely to save pages they'll want to come back to later, such as long articles and useful resources. If you want to get on the front page here, try compiling a list of tools that nobody could possibly read in a single sitting, or develop a tool that your readers will want to use regularly.

Niche Sites

Each of the most well-known popular social news sites has its own audience likes and dislikes; and as a site gains notoriety, it becomes increasingly difficult for content to go popular. If your site does not fit neatly into the profile of one of the big sites, you can try to create content that serves those niches while being only obliquely related to your business, or you can target one of the smaller, niche social news and voting sites. The following list is in no way exhaustive, but is meant to demonstrate the wide range of social news and bookmarking sites on the Web.

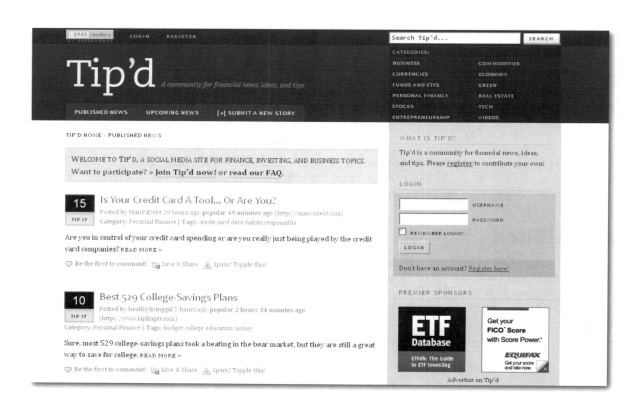

Figure 6-13. Tip'd is a great example of a smaller niche news and voting site.

Kirtsy (*http://kirtsy.com/*)

Referred to by some as "Digg for girls," Kirtsy has categories for crafts, parenting, fashion, and food. If your target audience is women, Kirtsy is a good place to start.

Tip'd (*http://tipd.com/*)

Tip'd focuses on finance, investing, and business (see Figure 6-13). Check it out if want to get your content in front of investors.

Sphinn (*http://sphinn.com/*)

The search and social media marketer's voting site, Sphinn (shown earlier in Figure 6-1) includes stories about SEO, PPC, domaining, and affiliate marketing.

Hacker News (*http://news.ycombinator.com/*)

Grown out of the funding firm Y Combinator, Hacker News carries technical content and "anything that a hacker might find interesting."

Care2 (*http://www.care2.com/*)

Care2's goal is to make the world a better place through green living. The site has news about a variety of causes, including animal welfare and environmental policy.

Takeaway Tips

- Social news and bookmarking sites are a great way to drive thousands of visitors and hundreds of links to a specific page.

- Set up your profile as completely as each site will allow.

- Write a compelling headline that tells visitors exactly what the article will offer them.

- Be sure ahead of time that your server can handle a huge spike in traffic.

- Use voting badges to make it easy to vote on your content.

- Consider the culture of each site and target your content appropriately.

CHAPTER 7

Ratings and Reviews

Introduction

According to an April 2009 Nielsen Media Research survey, 70% of consumers trust consumer opinions posted online, compared to the 62% who trust TV ads, 61% who trust newspaper ads, and 59% who trust magazine ads (see Figure 7-1). A 2007 study from Forrester showed that 19% of online consumers in the United States comment on blogs and post ratings and reviews on the Web at least once per month. It's likely that in the two years since that data was published, an even larger portion of the population is commenting on blogs and posting ratings regularly.

Users are already talking about your products, services, and brand online whether you're involved in the conversation or not, so you might as well join the discussion. Burying your head in the sand and ignoring rating sites will do you no good; every local business should have a presence on local review sites.

Users of other types of social media are typically more into socializing—they're simply having fun. But no one searches for a dentist in Boston to amuse herself; review-site visitors are in the midst of making a purchasing decision, and you should be there for them. Compared to other forms of online advertising, and even many other types of social media marketing, engaging review sites requires a much lower investment of time and money, making it one of the most cost-effective things you can do.

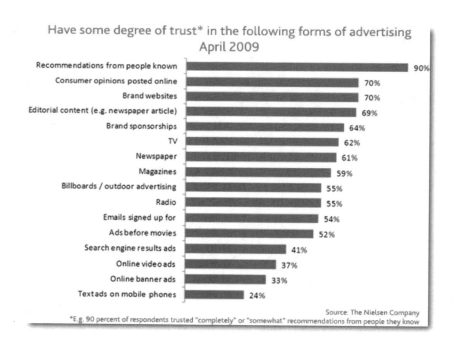

Figure 7-1. Customers trust online recommendations.

History

The behemoth of online retailers, Amazon.com, launched in 1994. The next year, Amazon added user reviews, giving everyone the power to anonymously review any book or product available on the site. A flurry of newspaper stories were printed detailing the horrors of nameless reviewers slathering libel on respected authors, but users loved it. In the same year, Citysearch.com was born as a local city website guide to tourist attractions, restaurants, museums, and retailers (see Figure 7-2). A natural environment for real feedback, it too soon incorporated user reviews.

In the 1979 Blake Edwards movie *10*, the main character says that on a scale of 1 to 10, Bo Derek's character is an 11, sparking a "scale of 1 to 10" fad. The idea spread to the Web in the late 1990s with a wave of "ratings" sites, including RateMyProfessors.com (see Figure 7-3), which allows students to submit reviews and numeric ratings of their teachers and professors, and HotOrNot.com, where users rate one another's attractiveness.

Many rating and review sites initially allowed users to post anonymously, but over time, most of them have incorporated a reputation system where users or their individual reviews can be rated on a scale of usefulness or accuracy. Recently, a new kind of review site has emerged that combines local ratings with social networking features. The popular site Yelp.com, launched in 2004, is an example of this type of site.

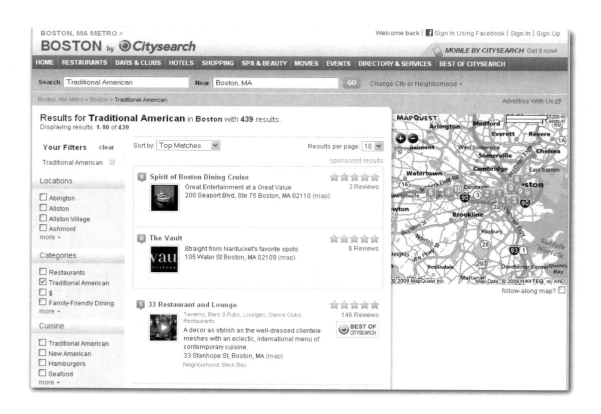

Figure 7-2. Like Amazon.com, Citysearch.com also incorporates user reviews.

Protocol

Ratings and review sites are some of the most useful for marketers, especially those with a local business focus. This section will introduce you to the common traits present across many of these types of sites.

Top Lists

Local review sites often have lists of the top businesses in certain categories or neighborhoods. When I'm browsing for a new place to eat or get a drink, I'll pick a category such as "romantic" or "French," and start at the top of the list. If I want to stay close to home, I'll check out the list for my neighborhood.

Search

The most common way users find listings on review sites is with search. Rankings are typically a combination of relevance (does the listing contain the search term?) and the number and quality of reviews. The popularity of search means it is important to include words and phrases that people may use to search for a business like yours; without them, nobody may ever find it.

Sock Puppets

A *sock puppet* is a form of web spam where an overzealous business owner sets up a bunch of fake accounts and cranks out sparkling reviews of his business, often while slamming his competition. Some owners will pay people to post positive reviews of their products. This is obviously very bad form and chances are good that you'll get caught; review sites have implemented algorithms designed to spot fraudulent activity. Getting caught in one of these attempts will be far worse than receiving a few organic bad reviews.

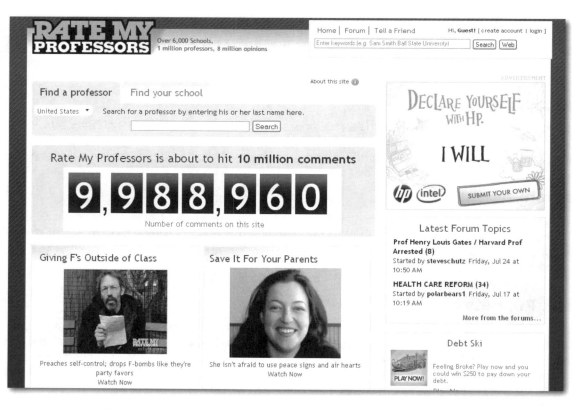

Figure 7-3. RateMyProfessors.com was one of the earliest rating sites.

Responding

Review sites generally have a mechanism that allows you, as a business owner or employee, to respond to reviews. Yelp (see Figure 7-4), TripAdvisor, Citysearch, and Superpages all support this functionality.

When responding to a review, keep a cool head. If a poster gets you upset, don't respond right away; step away from the computer for a while to calm down. A user's review is her perception of a business, and a subjective opinion can't be wrong. If a user has posted incorrect or grossly misleading information, you can correct her, but your responses shouldn't consist entirely of "You're Wrong!"

Ask the reviewer if there is anything specific you can do to make the situation right, try to fix her problem if you can, and offer a discount to entice her back to your business, after which she'll hopefully post a positive follow-up review. Your response will be there for the entire Web to read, likely for a very long time, so be sure it casts you and your business in a helpful, if sometimes imperfect, light rather than making you look rude and arrogant.

Most negative reviews are the result of poor communication between a customer and an owner, so the solution is to talk it out. Yelp makes it possible for you to contact a reviewer directly for a private response. This may be the advisable first step if you can easily solve someone's gripe. Try to work out the issue with the user and make her so happy that she edits her review without you needing to respond in public.

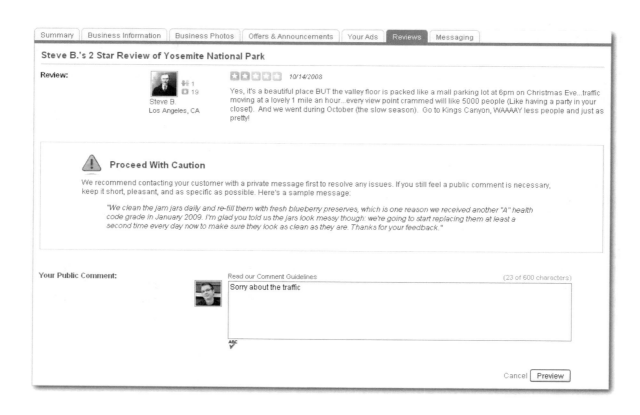

Figure 7-4. Yelp is one of the review sites where you can respond to a review.

Yelp

The largest local review directory on the Web, Yelp is a blend of social networking and ratings with a tight-knit community and a variety of tools for business owners.

Unlocking the Business Owner Account

I spoke with Luther Lowe, manager of Local Business Outreach for Yelp, and he recommended that the first thing you as a business owner should do is head to *https://biz.yelp.com/* and unlock your page. The process is intuitive and includes finding your business, setting up your account, and confirming that you own or work for the business in question.

Once you have unlocked your page, you can view activity graphs that show the level of traffic your page has gotten over the past few months or days, as well as post information about your business, including special offers and announcements. You'll also be able to respond either privately or publicly to reviews posted about your business.

Offers and Announcements

At the top of each business page on Yelp (under the location information), there is a box that owners can use to enter additional information, including offers or announcements of upcoming events (see Figure 7-5). This is a great spot to include sale information or offer Yelp users discounts on your products or services. Luther shared an example of a tennis coach who used this space to link to old testimonials and reviews of his lessons that his customers had written.

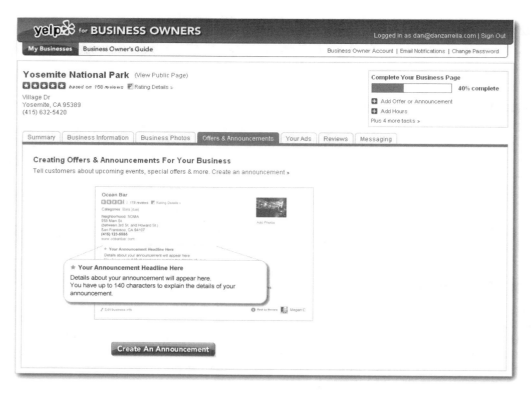

Figure 7-5. Yelp allows small business owners to post information about their business, including special offers and announcements.

Website Badges and Stickers

To encourage reviews of your business, you can post Yelp badges on your site, telling your visitors that you're on Yelp and directing them to your reviews (see Figure 7-6). Get the HTML code for these badges from your business owner account by clicking on the "Get Badges for Your Website" link.

Businesses that get a certain number of positive reviews sometimes get window stickers in the mail from Yelp that say "People Love Us on Yelp." You can—and should—display these at the entrance to your business to ensure that people know you're on Yelp.

Physical and website badges are subtle calls to action that can lead Yelp users to review your business. They also serve as social proof, telling even non-Yelpers that if a bunch of other people liked your products or services, they probably will, too.

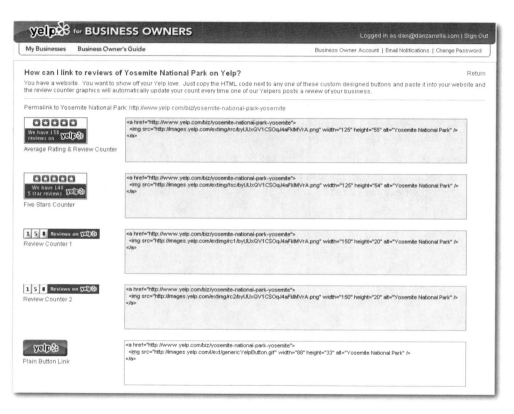

Figure 7-6. Yelp badges for your website.

Elite Yelp Squad

In most major U.S. cities, Yelp has created groups for its most active members, called Elite Yelp Squads. Members use their real names and photos on their profiles, and are known for posting lots of helpful and entertaining reviews. Yelp organizes networking events at local venues for elite squad members through community managers.

Hosting one of these events is a great idea if you can pull it off well—the word of mouth and positive review benefits would be priceless. To be considered, your business should have good reviews and you should contact the community manager for your region; you can reach this person by email at *<cityname>@yelp.com* (e.g., the email for the Boston manager would be *boston@yelp.com*).

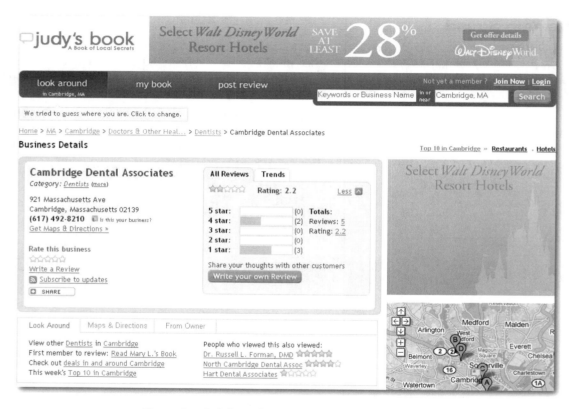

Figure 7-7. Judy's Book is another popular review site.

Other Sites

Although Yelp is currently the most popular local review site, the Web is home to a few other well-known review sites, too. You can apply most of the lessons you learn from working with Yelp to other sites. Also, don't forget that all social media sites can host reviews. Twitter is probably the most powerful review site that exists; here are some others:

Citysearch (*http://citysearch.com/*)

> Likely the oldest local review site, this was the leader in the space for many years and has only recently been overtaken by Yelp in terms of traffic.

Superpages (*http://www.superpages.com/*)

> Verizon's online Yellow Pages site allows users to review and rate listings on a 1–5 scale, and its search results are ranked by these ratings.

Insider Pages (*http://www.insiderpages.com/*)

> Billing itself as a local search service, Insider Pages includes reviews and images from users, and offers business owners management tools, similar to Yelp.

TripAdvisor (*http://www.tripadvisor.com/*)

> TripAdvisor focuses on travel-related issues and features reviews and user-submitted photos of hotels, resorts, and vacation packages.

Judy's Book (*http://www.judysbook.com/*)

> This site's tagline is "A Book of Local Secrets," and it offers the standard reviewing and rating fare (see Figure 7-7).

Takeaway Tips

- Review sites are the most cost-effective form of social marketing for small, local businesses.

- Make sure your listings on review sites include plenty of relevant keywords so that people can find you in search results.

- Respond to negative reviews, but always remain calm and try to resolve the issue.

- Unlock your business page at Yelp.

- Post stickers and badges on your websites and physical locations to encourage more reviews.

CHAPTER 8

Forums

Introduction

Arguably the oldest type of social media, forums are a modern version of community bulletin boards. The focus of these kinds of sites is discussion. Users will make posts to them and others will respond. Become a valuable and respected member in one of these communities by answering questions and contributing useful information.

Unlike other types of social media, where there are a few major sites, there are thousands of popular forums on the Web, each centered on a single topic or community. Find the ones that are relevant to your business and engage them, but be careful, as forum users typically dislike obvious advertising.

History

In 1979, a distributed communication system called Usenet was created as a joint project between the University of North Carolina and Duke University. It was a type of mailing list that allowed users to post an article that other people could respond to. Conversations on Usenet were called *message threads* because of the linear post-and-response pattern. It is one of the oldest social networks still in existence.

Over the next few decades, Usenet spawned much of what we know as the Internet today—Tim Berners-Lee actually announced the launch of the World Wide Web on Usenet. Much of the slang we use today began on Usenet, and a strong argument could be made that web spam first happened there, too.

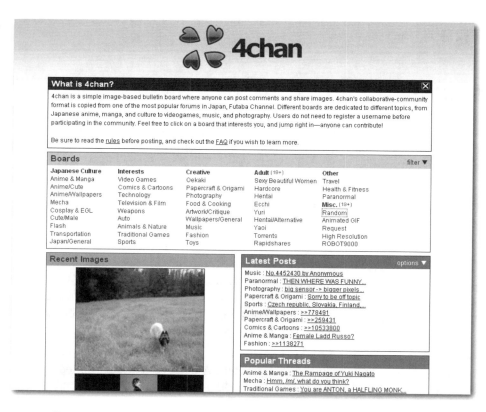

Figure 8-1. 4Chan is one of the most popular English-language forums.

Modern threaded discussions happen on sites known as *forums*. Unlike social networks, there is no single dominant site in the United States—instead, there are several hundred fairly popular forums. One of the largest in English is 4Chan (see Figure 8-1). Conceived as America's answer to Japan's hugely popular anime discussion forum 2Channel, 4Chan has spawned some of the largest and most pervasive recent Internet sensations, including LOLcats and Rickrolling.

Forums since Usenet have had insular communities with inside jokes and jargon, and new members— known as *newbies* or *n00bs*—are often ridiculed (especially on the more elitist sites such as 4Chan). Marketers should be aware of this and dedicate much time to developing a deep understanding of each community's individual rules and culture before jumping in.

Protocol

Forums are one of the oldest forms of web-based social media, and each one has its own culture and rules. Most forum platforms include a number of software features. This section will cover those features.

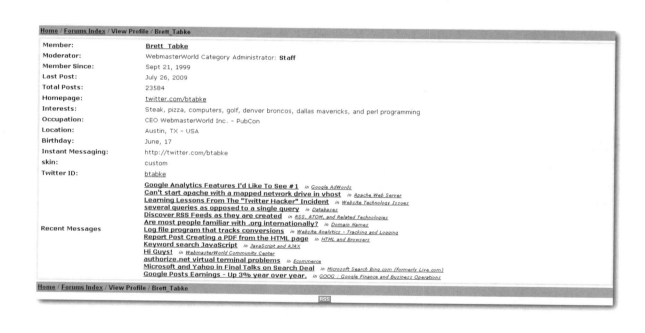

Figure 8-2. A forum profile typically includes a short bio and some simple personal information.

Profiles

Your profile on a forum is a representation of who you are. You'll typically be able to write a short bio about yourself and provide some simple personal information (see Figure 8-2).

The most important part of profile setup is your *avatar*. This is an image that will be displayed next to every post you make, so choose it wisely. If your account will represent you personally, you should choose a good personal photo for your avatar, perhaps the same image you use on Twitter. Otherwise, you should make your avatar an extension of the brand you're promoting, by using a logo or similar colors. But remember: profiles are best used for individuals, not companies.

Lurking

I know it sounds creepy, but it's not. *Lurking* simply means spending a lot of time reading posts and observing how the community operates before you start contributing. This is a good idea, and forum rules and site owners usually suggest it.

Posting

You communicate on a forum by writing posts. A *post* is traditionally a short text-based piece of content, but some types of forum software allow you to upload and attach images as well. A post will be labeled with the date and time of creation, as well as the poster's username, avatar, and possibly some kind of reputation value.

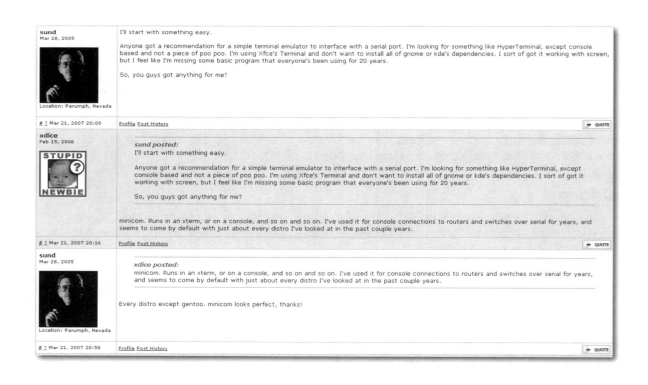

Figure 8-3. A forum thread lists posts in chronological order from earliest to most recent.

Threads

Conversations on forums are organized into *threads*, with posts listed in chronological order from earliest to most recent (see Figure 8-3). The first post—called the *original post* or *OP*—is at the top of the thread, with response posts listed below it. Forums are divided into categories, and threads are listed on each category's page, with the threads that have had new posts most recently at the top.

When replying to a thread, stay relevant to the OP. Changing the topic or point of a thread is known as *thread hijacking* and is frowned upon.

Before you start a new thread, familiarize yourself with the rules and community of the forum—lurk for a while before doing this. And search the forum for similar posts to be sure you're not duplicating an existing thread. Be especially careful when posting marketing content. Ensure that the rules of the forum allow this, and remember that even if they do, marketing content might not be well received by the community. Creativity here will help get your message across in a palatable form.

Moderators and Administrators

The owner(s) and other trusted individuals from a forum's community are known as *moderators* (mods) or *administrators* (admins). Their job is to prevent spam, enforce forum rules, keep discussions on topic, and settle disputes between members.

As a new community member, and especially as one who is interested in marketing through a forum, you should be very nice to mods and admins, since you'll need them to like you. If you can become friends by sending out some gifts or doing favors for them, do it.

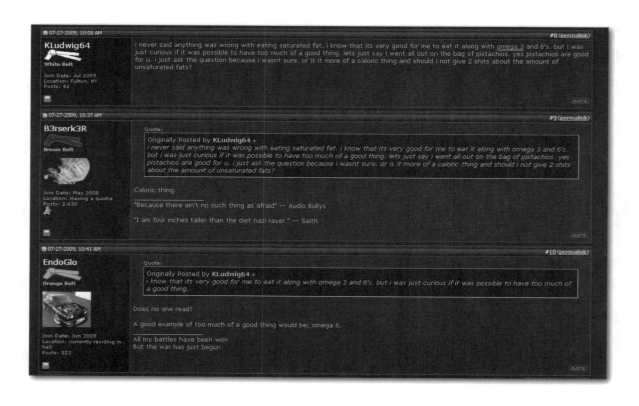

Figure 8-4. The lines of text below the horizontal line in each post are signatures.

Signature

Some types of forum software contain a feature known as a *signature* (*sig* for short). These are short text or image messages that are appended to all of your posts (see Figure 8-4). These can be very useful for you as a marketer, but you'll need to read the forum's rules regarding signature conduct—some forums allow banner ads or commercial links, and some do not. Be clear in your understanding of what is acceptable and what is not.

Your signature will appear on every one of your posts, so don't make it too long, as it gets annoying for other users to be forced to scroll through it. If the forum allows images, this can be a good place to introduce some of your company's brand, especially if you're following best practices and your avatar is a picture of you.

Reputation

A profile will often be assigned some value as a measurement of its reputation on that forum. In some cases, reputation is calculated by the sheer number of posts you've made on the forum; in other cases, it is a measurement of how much other people have liked your contributions. If the forum supports reputation, it will be displayed next to your avatar on your posts.

On some forums, members will be assigned levels based on their reputation points. A martial arts forum I'm fond of gives out different color belts.

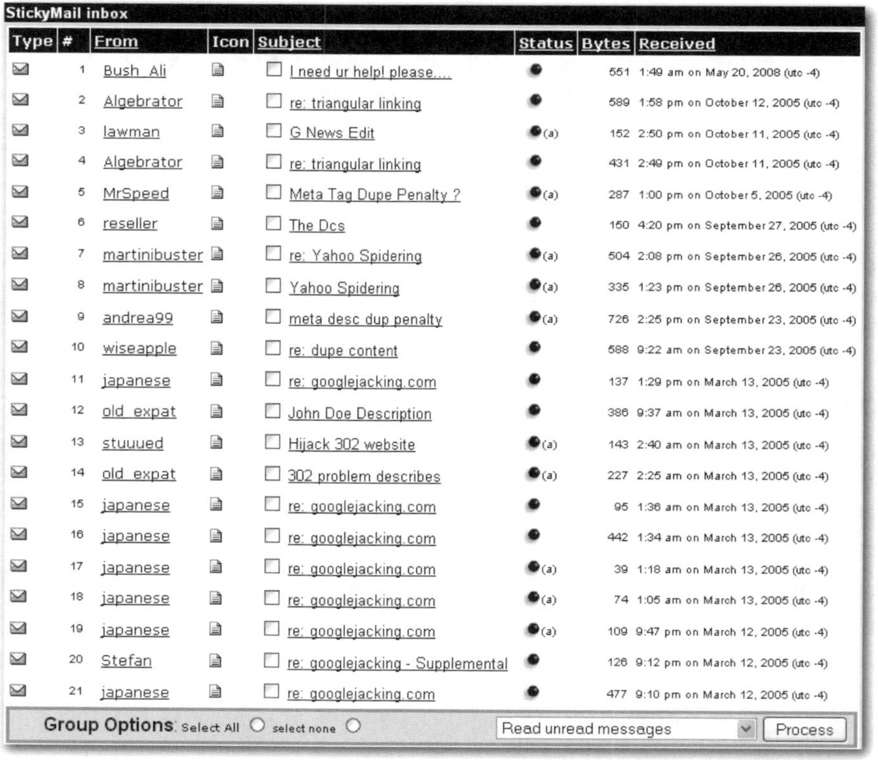

Type	#	From	Icon	Subject	Status	Bytes	Received
✉	1	Bush_Ali	📄	☐ I need ur help! please....	●	551	1:49 am on May 20, 2008 (utc -4)
✉	2	Algebrator	📄	☐ re: triangular linking	●	589	1:58 pm on October 12, 2005 (utc -4)
✉	3	lawman	📄	☐ G News Edit	●(a)	152	2:50 pm on October 11, 2005 (utc -4)
✉	4	Algebrator	📄	☐ re: triangular linking	●	431	2:49 pm on October 11, 2005 (utc -4)
✉	5	MrSpeed	📄	☐ Meta Tag Dupe Penalty ?	●(a)	287	1:00 pm on October 5, 2005 (utc -4)
✉	6	reseller	📄	☐ The Dcs	●	150	4:20 pm on September 27, 2005 (utc -4)
✉	7	martinibuster	📄	☐ re: Yahoo Spidering	●(a)	504	2:08 pm on September 26, 2005 (utc -4)
✉	8	martinibuster	📄	☐ Yahoo Spidering	●(a)	335	1:23 pm on September 26, 2005 (utc -4)
✉	9	andrea99	📄	☐ meta desc dup penalty	●(a)	726	2:25 pm on September 23, 2005 (utc -4)
✉	10	wiseapple	📄	☐ re: dupe content	●	588	9:22 am on September 23, 2005 (utc -4)
✉	11	japanese	📄	☐ re: googlejacking.com	●	137	1:29 pm on March 13, 2005 (utc -4)
✉	12	old_expat	📄	☐ John Doe Description	●	386	9:37 am on March 13, 2005 (utc -4)
✉	13	stuuued	📄	☐ Hijack 302 website	●(a)	143	2:40 pm on March 13, 2005 (utc -4)
✉	14	old_expat	📄	☐ 302 problem describes	●(a)	227	2:25 pm on March 13, 2005 (utc -4)
✉	15	japanese	📄	☐ re: googlejacking.com	●	95	1:36 am on March 13, 2005 (utc -4)
✉	16	japanese	📄	☐ re: googlejacking.com	●	442	1:34 am on March 13, 2005 (utc -4)
✉	17	japanese	📄	☐ re: googlejacking.com	●(a)	39	1:18 am on March 13, 2005 (utc -4)
✉	18	japanese	📄	☐ re: googlejacking.com	●(a)	74	1:05 am on March 13, 2005 (utc -4)
✉	19	japanese	📄	☐ re: googlejacking.com	●(a)	109	9:47 pm on March 12, 2005 (utc -4)
✉	20	Stefan	📄	☐ re: googlejacking - Supplemental	●	126	9:12 pm on March 12, 2005 (utc -4)
✉	21	japanese	📄	☐ re: googlejacking.com	●	477	9:10 pm on March 12, 2005 (utc -4)

Group Options: Select All ○ select none ○   [Read unread messages ▾] [Process]

Figure 8-5. Forums allow you to send PMs to other members. Here's an example of a forum inbox.

Private Messaging

Like social networks, forums allow you to send private messages (PMs), which function much like emails, to other members (see Figure 8-5). If you want to start developing a relationship with an important user or mod, send him a PM introducing yourself and offering whatever help you can. It bears repeating that sending a ton of these is considered spam, and it's more useful to keep your content in the public eye anyway. When in doubt, post your messages on a thread rather than a PM.

Trolls and Flaming

A *flame* is a post designed to do nothing other than incite heated reactions. Flame wars typically ensue after emotional discussions on things people are especially passionate about, such as operating systems, sports teams, politics, and religion. As you get to know a community, you'll start to understand which topics to tiptoe around.

A *troll* is a person whose only intention on a forum is to annoy people. Typically a new and faceless member, the troll specializes in pushing buttons and stirring up trouble. He delights when you lose your temper, and when he finds out that you work for a specific company, he'll be taking shots at your products. He feeds on attention and emotion. The only good way to defeat a troll is to ignore him; many forums have a "don't feed the trolls" rule. There is a difference between a troll and a good member criticizing your business; learn to spot the difference, and address the legitimate concerns of the latter.

Rank	Board name and description		Posts	Members
1	**Gaia Online** Anime roleplaying community	phpBB	1606422186	18555289
2	**4chan** Japanese culture message board		291533472	28362
3	**d2jsp** Diablo 2 video game forums	custom	212562816	483548
4	**IGN boards** General video gaming message boards	IGNBoards	198202697	1255254
5	**Nexopia** Picture rating, sex and relationships forums	custom	182602864	1424092
6	**FaceTheJury** Real life picture rating forums	custom	155477733	552000
7	**Vault Network boards** Role playing games discussion boards	IGNBoards	121577397	626203
8	**Offtopic.com** General discussion forums	vBulletin	118706504	208355
9	**Something Awful** General discussion forums	vBulletin	89612862	131244
10	**BuddyPic** Picture rating message board	custom	72366965	1587120
11	**PBNation** Paintball related message boards	vBulletin	57405617	478677
12	**VW vortex forums** Volkswagen and related car brands discussion boards	zeroforum	54875353	472982
13	**Christian Forums** Christian-based forum and online community	vBulletin	47768404	224279
14	**Bodybuilding.com** Bodybuilding and fitness related forums	vBulletin	41726505	1731261
15	**PinoyExchange** Online Filipino community	vBulletin	36990724	325639
16	**Fan Forum** Community for celebrities fans	vBulletin	35731362	178688
17	**Honda tech** Honda cars enthusiasts forums	zeroforum	34644340	297178
18	**Digital Spy** General digital entertainment community	vBulletin	34090321	335321
19	**Disney discussion forums** Disney trip planning forums	vBulletin	30688189	226990
20	**Corvette Forum** Chevrolet corvette forum	vBulletin	30462436	221880

Figure 8-6. The most popular forums on the Web boast large numbers of posts and members.

Research

The first step in forum marketing is to identify relevant and popular forums to join. A good place to start is a search on forum tracking and ranking sites such as the following:

- *http://boardreader.com/*
- *http://www.big-boards.com/*
- *http://boardtracker.com/*

Enter a few keywords about the product or company you're trying to promote, and click through to find related forums. Look for signs of popularity, and check how many members and threads it has and how recently they've been posted to. Focus on the large and active sites. Figure 8-6 lists the most popular forums on the Web.

While marketing a geek dating website, I created a promotion centered on a lip gloss giveaway to attract women. I was frustrated with many social media sites, since they were full of twentysomething guys, so I stopped promoting it for a while. When I logged in to check the site's traffic a few weeks later, I was shocked to see a huge uptick in visits coming from a bunch of different forums. It turns out that a member of a small "freebie" forum had found my offer and posted about it, and within hours it was reposted to hundreds of other sites. My efforts prior to that had created an initial spike in traffic that faded off after a few days, but this time the hits kept coming for weeks.

Don't underestimate the power of networks of niche forums to drive impressive numbers of visitors to your site, and remember that the best promotion doesn't come from you, but your fans.

Forum Rules

Sunday, January 1, 2006 Update by Rich "Lowtax" Kyanka

Pages: 1 2 3 Next page »

Herein lie the rules for the Something Awful Forums. Please visit our support FAQ page if you are experiencing any technical problems, problems with an order, problems with your account, or if you are thinking of contacting us for any other reason at all. Most questions can be answered there if you just READ IT. And now, on to the rules!

Make sure you are familiar with the rules below. Memorize them. Read them daily if you have to. They are guidelines you must follow in order to keep your account privileges. If you break a rule, you will likely be punished. Punishment can be a temporary or permanent loss of privileges. Most users have been around for many years and not had any problems. This is because they know the rules!

A Message To the Newbies!

We here on the Something Awful Forums are very elitist and strict assholes. We pride ourselves on running one of the most entertaining and troll-free forums on the internet. This is accomplished by charging a $10 fee to filter out folks not serious about adhering to the rules, and banning those who manage to slip through and break them. We are very serious about keeping our forums clean and troll-free, so please consider your account an investment and treat it accordingly. Read the rules, use common sense, and help keep the SA Forums the best message board on the internet!

General Conduct

Lurk before posting! We cannot stress this enough. Each forum pretty much makes it clear from its name and description what is acceptable in there or not. Be sure you have the appropriate forum before posting. If there is no forum dedicated to the topic you wish to discuss, use General Bullshit. Do NOT post porn or any "questionable" material in GBS; if you would be uncomfortable viewing it at work, do not post it there. Keep all disgusting pics in FYAD. Additionally, please check to see if your post is a redux (it has already been posted before by another forum member).

> **Before you post:** Before posting, please ask yourself the following question: **"Am I making a post which is either funny, informative, or interesting on any level?"**
>
> If you can answer "yes" to this, then please post. If you cannot, then refrain from posting. If you post anyway, the mods will probably gas your thread, automatically awarding you a 15-minute probation.
>
> **Before you reply:** Before replying, please ask yourself the following question: **"Does my reply offer**

Figure 8-7. Be sure to read forum rules.

Engaging

When you find a forum that you'd like to start working with, set up an account. Reputation systems are often based in part on account age, so you'll want to create yours as soon as possible—but don't start posting right away.

Before you even think about contributing to a new forum, spend some time lurking to learn about the forum's culture and community. Some forums don't allow members to post links to their own sites, and some forbid promotion or marketing of any kind. Read the rules and get to know which members are well known and trusted. Forums can be a minefield of unspoken rules and social taboos, and one wrong step by a marketer can be crippling to her reputation (see Figure 8-7).

There are a bunch of "forum marketing" services that the lazy marketer may be tempted to hire; resist these. Outsourcing your forum marketing is an easy way to wreck your reputation, as the vast majority of these services will be creating hundreds of accounts on as many different sites, only to post blatant advertisements devoid of any value to you or the forums.

Once you've gotten to know the lay of the land, you'll know if and when an introductory post is acceptable. If it is, do it and do it well. Be transparent about what company you work for and what your role is; if you're a marketing person, admit it. Highlight your unique skills and knowledge that will be useful to the community, and make a commitment to never spam or blatantly promote your wares. Make sure other members know you're approachable and that you appreciate feedback.

Figure 8-8. In this example, a forum user is asking for advice. Marketers should be all over this kind of post.

Your modus operandi in a forum should be to provide value (see Figure 8-8), answer as many questions as you can, and be as helpful as possible. Be consistent in your forum marketing efforts; once you've decided a certain site is worth your while, dedicate an amount of time every week or day to it and post regularly. Don't be a hit-and-run poster.

I asked Brett Tabke, founder of WebmasterWorld, one of the largest marketing communities on the Web, how marketers should approach forums. His advice was to remember that you can only reach out to people who want to be reached, and that by serving the community rather than promoting your brand, you can earn its respect. He also suggested that you get in the habit of starting quality threads as opposed to just replying to existing ones.

Regardless of the site's rules about promotion, you should not spam any forum. Avoid outright product pitches, and definitely don't post the same message multiple times on the same site.

Forums can be full of personal politics and negative sentiments, and you should avoid getting embroiled in them at all costs. Do not be caught bad-mouthing your competition or other members of the community. If you don't like the people you're communicating with, just leave. Brett says that the best way for members to deal with trolls and flame wars (see Figure 8-9) is to simply ignore them.

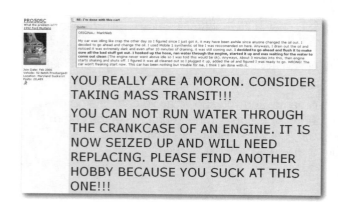

Figure 8-9. Beware of trolls and flame wars.

Figure 8-10. An empty forum is a sad-looking place.

Should You Start Your Own Forum?

One of the early bibles of social marketing was *The Cluetrain Manifesto* by Rick Levine et al. (Basic Books). In it, the authors suggest that companies should sponsor forums centered on their products or the communities they serve. A forum built and run by your company—if it succeeds—can do wonders for your social marketing. But that is a big *if*.

The decision to start a forum should not be taken lightly. Forums represent large investments of time and energy, and require a fair amount of technical ability to set up, design, and maintain. As it begins to grow, the forum will require an ever-increasing amount of effort to moderate and support.

Beyond the time it will take to build a forum, a considerable amount of marketing effort is also needed to attract and retain a viable community. If there are already popular forums in your niche—and this is true for most categories—this will become even more of an uphill battle, and your efforts will best be spent becoming a respected member of existing sites as opposed to trying to start from scratch. As Figure 8-10 shows, you don't want an empty forum.

If you are determined to start your own forum, make sure you do your homework before beginning. Research your market to identify existing forums (if you find large ones, reread my earlier advice). Have a robust understanding of what your company can offer a community that it can't get elsewhere. For instance, do you have inside information or unmatched expertise and experience? A vintage car restoration shop could start a forum with the goal of answering questions about the personal projects of its members, building thought leadership in the industry, and forming relationships with old-car enthusiasts. As another example, the popular purse forum shown in Figure 8-11 allows members to post links to handbags for sale on the Web to be authenticated as fake or real.

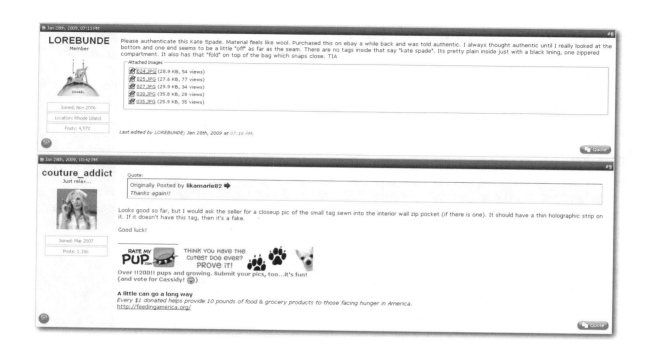

Figure 8-11. Users can ask for expert advice authenticating designer handbags on this forum.

Brett said that prospective forum admins should read everything they can about forums and communities on the Web and study other sites in their niche. He also pointed out that you shouldn't expect overnight success; good communities take years to build.

A number of options are available for software on which to build your forum, and many are open source. Unless you are a technical person, you should leave these decisions to the technically savvy person who will be building and maintaining the forum. If you don't have a developer or IT resources available, you should be looking for some before moving ahead with your forum.

Here are some of the more popular software options available for building a forum:

vBulletin (*http://www.vbulletin.com/*)

vBulletin is a commercial forum software package that runs many of the Web's largest message boards. It is written in PHP and uses a MySQL database, meaning that it runs on Linux or Unix. According to Big-Boards.com, vBulletin is the most popular forum software.

Invision Power Board (*http://www.invisionpower.com/*)

Invision is listed as the second most popular forum software package. It is open source and built on PHP and MySQL.

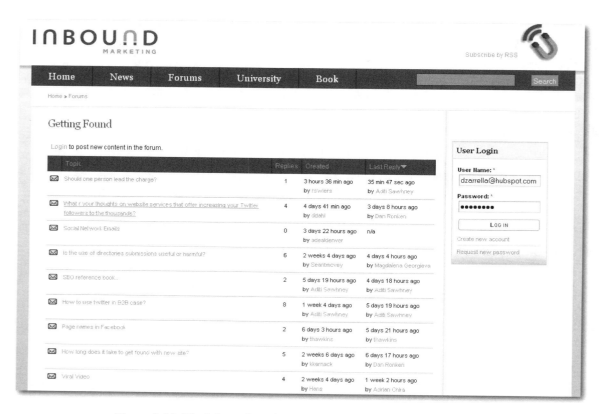

Figure 8-12. The InboundMarketing.com forums are built on Drupal.

phpBB (*http://www.phpbb.com/*)

phpBB is an open source forum system that has been in development since 2000. It runs on PHP and MySQL, and Big-Boards.com ranks it as the third most popular package.

Drupal

One of the most popular open source content management systems (CMSs), Drupal can be configured to create nearly any kind of community site, and includes a robust forum system. It is written in PHP and runs best on a Linux or Unix server.

At the time of this writing, we at HubSpot are in the process of launching our own community site for marketers—InboundMarketing.com—that is built on Drupal (see Figure 8-12). The forum is the most popular section of the site at this point. We have several development teams in-house, as development, design, and maintenance require a significant investment of time.

Takeaway Tips

- Forums are a great way to build a reputation in a specific niche online.

- Lurk, lurk, and lurk some more; get to know the community before you start posting.

- Contribute, don't pitch. Hard selling won't work.

- Become a part of the community; don't be a hit-and-run poster.

- Starting your own forum can be rewarding, but it is a ton of work, so be sure to do your homework.

CHAPTER 9
Virtual Worlds

Introduction

Promised by science fiction for decades, large-scale virtual worlds have begun to emerge that are centered on games and social activities. Many extremely popular worlds are games, such as *World of Warcraft*, but the social marketing possibilities in these worlds are often very limited. Therefore, this chapter will focus on Second Life, where marketers have a variety of techniques at their disposal.

Building places and objects in Second Life requires a technical prowess that is likely too advanced for a new user. If you decide that a virtual world presence would be valuable to your company, a number of companies and individuals can assist you in creating one.

Figure 9-1. Snow Crash is one of the most influential novels in technology's history.

History

The 1992, Neal Stephenson's cyberpunk novel *Snow Crash* (Bantam Spectra) inspired web technology in much the same way that the Beatles inspired rock music (see Figure 9-1). The idea behind Google Earth, the use of avatars on computers, and my own interest in social and viral marketing all sprang from different parts of Stephenson's classic work.

The most talked about element in the book was the Metaverse, a virtual reality view of what the Internet could be. In the story, wealthy, famous, and intellectually gifted users logged in with a pair of 3D goggles and socialized in elite and exclusive clubs. Constructed around a single street encircling a featureless planet, the Metaverse was constrained to a stringent set of physical rules modeled on reality. You could be only as tall as you were in real life, for example, and there was no teleporting—only walking, driving, and public transport.

Many multiplayer games have emerged since *Snow Crash* was published, but these gaming worlds are entirely created and controlled by the designer, with users playing parts like they would in interactive movies. The Metaverse is a set of programming interfaces, a platform upon which users can build their own realities.

In 2003, the virtual world known as Second Life was launched. Founder Philip Rosedale envisioned it to be the real Metaverse, where users could socialize, buy and sell virtual goods, and learn. In this version, you can teleport and fly, and the geography is far more complex, but almost everything else is the same as the book. Because Second Life is user-created and socially driven, there are far more marketing opportunities than in a game-based world such as *World of Warcraft* or *Sims Online*.

Figure 9-2. The Second Life sign-on screen is where you can sign up for an account.

Second Life

The dominant virtual world today, Second Life is owned by Linden Lab, with founding visionary Philip Rosedale serving as current chairman of the board of directors. The user demographics resemble average web users, and Second Life "residents" spend widely varying amounts of time logged in or "in-world." I sat down with John Lester, the operations director of the Boston offices of Linden Lab, and he told me that the most important thing for a marketer who is new to Second Life to know is that it is not the Web, but a unique medium accessed *through* the Web. You're going to need to spend some time in-world to get to know the platform and the community.

John said that even Linden Lab doesn't know exactly how people are going to be using the platform, so you shouldn't worry if you don't, either. Companies such as IBM have leveraged Second Life to build internal tools to allow their globally dispersed workforce to gather and communicate, whereas Dell built an oversized computer that users can walk through, either alone or with other people, sharing their experiences along the way.

Figure 9-2 shows a screenshot of the Second Life sign-on screen.

Linden Dollars

Second Life financial transactions are conducted in Linden dollars (L$). Sold by Linden Lab for roughly L$265 per U.S. dollar, they can also be turned back into real-world money through Linden Lab and third-party brokers. Buildings in-world can be purchased for amounts equivalent to tens of U.S. dollars, and automobiles for a few bucks.

Figure 9-3. Here's what I look like in Second Life.

Your Avatar

The physical representation of you in Second Life is your avatar: a 3D figure composed of a skin, body shape, and clothes. Second Life provides basic tools that allow you to customize your appearance, but for best results, you should look into buying one of the professionally produced sets that are widely available and provide endless customization options, from zombies to spacemen—even normal, every-day people (see Figure 9-3).

Real Estate

Linden Lab sells processing power on its servers through the metaphor of land; there is a robust real estate market operated by residents as well. At least one resident has made more than 1 million, real-world U.S. dollars buying and selling Second Life real estate, proving that it is, indeed, big business.

There are two types of land: mainland and estate land. Mainland is created only at the discretion of Linden Lab, whereas estate land is disconnected from the rest of the world and can be created when-ever someone buys it. Purchase prices vary on size and type of land and can exceed several thousand U.S. dollars. Monthly fees are also charged to those who own land, ranging from US$5 to US$295.

A common marketing avenue is for a company to buy some land and build an office or visitor center. Unless these are interactive and social, inviting user participation, they quickly turn into empty ghost towns and can be expensive in terms of setup and maintenance.

Groups

Second Life features functionality that allows users to create groups that can own land and objects. Group members can communicate with each other and hold virtual events. Groups must have at least

Figure 9-4. Second Life's search functionality is one of the primary ways for residents to find people, places, groups, and services in-world.

two members to remain active. Each user can be a member of up to 25 groups, so experienced residents will only join groups that provide a lot of value to them. When a user joins your group and sets it as her current "active" group, a title you define is displayed above her avatar name. Clever, eye-catching titles are appreciated by users and will encourage them to "wear" yours more often, increasing your exposure to the world. Several systems exist to offer the communication functionality of a group without the expenditure of a user group slot, allowing broadcast messages to your subscribers as well as sending along in-world objects, graphics, or landmarks. These subscription services are popular with users, especially power users with no group slots to spare.

Teleporting

Most travel in-world is done by point-to-point teleportation, meaning that advertising through banners and billboards is essentially useless in terms of the real-world metaphor of the roadside billboard. If someone is bored somewhere, he can instantly be somewhere else—your competition is always only a few clicks away. You facilitate visitor travel to your site by providing landmarks, which are like World Wide Web bookmarks, and allow the user to easily return to your site. Landmarks can be made by the user through the viewer client, but if you provide the landmarks yourself, you can keep track of how many you have handed out, thus giving you a picture of how engaged your users are by noting how many might like to return!

Search

One of the primary ways for Second Life residents to find people, places, groups, and services in-world is through the built-in search functionality (see Figure 9-4). Results are ranked by relevance to the search term entered and a traffic score. Simply put, the more people that frequent a specific place, the higher it will appear in the search results. The easiest way to help people find you is to write a good parcel description with well-chosen keywords relevant to your site.

Figure 9-5. IBM built and sponsored the Ballet Pixelle Theatre.

SLurl (Second Life URL)

Linden Lab maintains a web-based linking system, in which users can create HTTP links that allow you to instantly teleport to a specific location from a link in a web browser. If your company has built a presence in-world, a *SLurl* can be used to link visitors from your website—as well as from your other social media efforts—to your Second Life offices. SLurls can, for example, be packed into a shortened URL and posted with an announcement of an in-world event on your Twitter account. Linden Lab provides brand usage advice as well as logos you can use on your pages at its website, *http://secondlife.com/corporate/brand/insl/*.

You Don't Have to Do Everything Yourself

A point John made emphatically is that marketers and individuals in Second Life shouldn't feel like they have to do everything themselves; a great strategy is to find something that residents are doing successfully and that fits with your core values, and then sponsor it.

For instance, a popular group in-world, Ballet Pixelle, organizes some well-attended dance performances and was struggling to find a venue that could keep up with its growing audiences. IBM is known in the real world for sponsoring the arts, and when it heard of Ballet Pixelle's difficulties, the computer company built a theatre for them. Now when the troupe delivers their 90-minute shows, viewers are being subtly exposed to the IBM brand (see Figure 9-5).

Figure 9-6. Stores and boutiques where you can buy just about anything are available in-world. This is an image of the now-closed Second Life American Apparel store at night.

Building things is a pretty complex task to do well, so if there's something specific you need or want, there's a pretty good chance someone else has already created it; if not, you can easily find someone who is a wizard at building and scripting in-world. Linden Lab maintains a directory of service providers that range from full-service solution agencies to individual contractors, and some of these providers have been vetted by Linden Lab to ensure the reliable delivery of services. The company also owns XStreetSL.com, an Amazon-for-Second-Life marketplace where third parties sell virtual goods. There are also countless stores and boutiques in-world, where you can buy everything from clothes to cars to furniture (see Figure 9-6).

Engagement Versus Volume

Perhaps the most important thing that John said in my conversation with him is that when you compare a Second Life presence with a website, you need to understand that with Second Life, you won't be getting millions of eyeballs, but the people who do interact with you in-world will be much more engaged. A visitor to your website may spend a few minutes interacting with your brand, whereas a visitor to your island or virtual store might spend an hour or more.

Takeaway Tips

- Virtual worlds offer an opportunity to engage your audience in immersive experiences.
- Spend a lot of time in-world to understand the culture before you start promoting.
- Second Life is a tricky place to support marketing efforts; find an experienced resident to help you.
- Customize, customize, customize. Ensure that your land, avatar, and objects reflect your brand.
- Find already successful things in-world and leverage them like IBM did with Ballet Pixelle.

CHAPTER 10

Strategy, Tactics, and Practice

Introduction

Strategy and tactics are inseparable. You can't design a strategy without deep, firsthand knowledge of the tactics you'll be using, and tactics are aimless without a strategy to guide them. In the preceding eight chapters, I introduced you to eight different categories of social media tools and how you can leverage them for marketing. Now it's time to start thinking about them as parts of your whole marketing mix.

If you've been doing other kinds of marketing for your business, you'll have some understanding of your "brand" and positioning in your market. This is your vision, and your social media strategy should fit with your established identity. But don't let the dead hand of history limit the new ideas you're willing to try out or the risks you're willing to take. One of the worst mistakes a new social media marketer will make is to apply the same strategies from the offline broadcast world to the social Web.

Before you launch into a social media conversation, listen. As you do when joining a new forum, lurk in every medium you're going to enter to get a sense of the rules and customs, and of who the influential people are.

Figure 10-1. I entered "zarrella" for the keyword I wanted to monitor in Yahoo! Pipes.

Monitoring

Whether you're a local business or an international brand, chances are good that people are already talking about you on the Web. But before you can get involved in those conversations, you have to start listening. You can't respond if you don't know what is being said, where it is being said, and who is saying it. Monitoring social media is an ongoing process, and you should use multiple systems to be sure nothing slips through the cracks—the right (or wrong) story can come from anywhere and blow up in your face. You don't want to get caught off guard.

The first tools you should be using allow you to search for your name, business name, and product names; you should then subscribe to the search results via RSS. Set up an account on Google Reader (or your feed reader of choice) with these feeds, and check the account once or twice a day. For simplicity, I mashed up all the sources in the following list using Yahoo! Pipes, so you can just enter your keyword into the form at *http://pipes.yahoo.com/danzarrella/monitoring* and subscribe to one RSS of the results. Do this once for each word you'd like to monitor. I recommend your company name, your product names, your name, and key employees' names.

- Technorati Search
- IceRocket Blog Search
- Google News Search
- Twitter Search
- Google Video Search
- Digg Search
- BoardReader.com Search
- BoardTracker.com Search
- SocialMention.com "All" Search
- Reddit Search
- BackType Blog Comment Search

Figure 10-1 shows the results I received after entering the keyword *zarrella*.

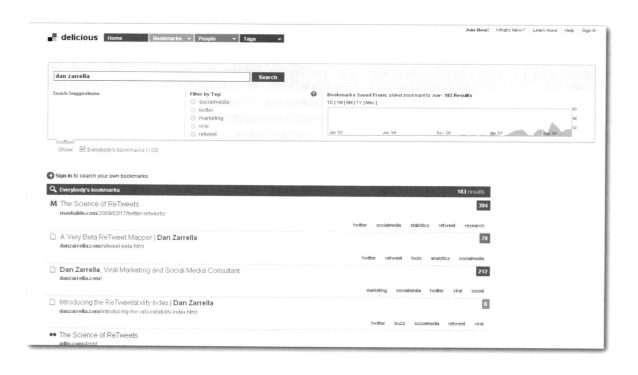

Figure 10-2. Delicious doesn't offer feeds of keyword searches, but you should visit it regularly and conduct a manual search.

The sources in the preceding list are a great start, but there are a few important sites that don't offer feeds of keyword searches. Visit these sites on a regular basis—perhaps once a week—and do a manual search:

- Delicious (see Figure 10-2)

- StumbleUpon

- Smaller social news and bookmarking sites in your niche

- LinkedIn Answers

Google offers a free service called Google Alerts that will send you an email whenever a new result appears in the search listing for certain keywords. Set up alerts on the names you're monitoring, as this will help you catch anything else that gets through the rest of your searches.

Don't forget to monitor your industry, niche, and competitors' keywords. This way, you can learn what problems your potential audience has with existing products, what features they wish they had, and what they love most about your competitors, so you can stay ahead of the game and are better prepared to ward off future problems. Think of social media as your focus group. When I spoke with Jennifer Zeszut, CEO of Scout Labs, she described monitoring strategy as a hierarchy of needs, with crisis management at the bottom and market intelligence near the top (see Figure 10-3).

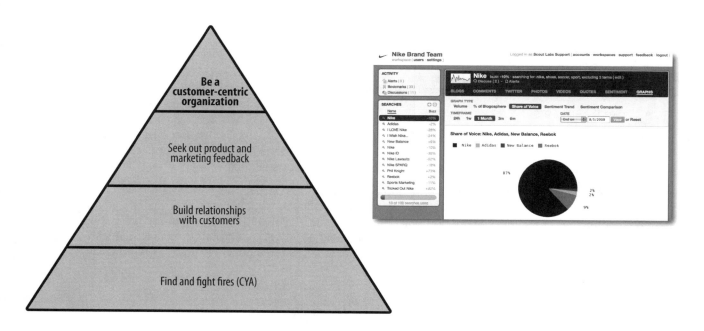

Figure 10-3. In Scout Labs' social media hierarchy of needs, crisis management is at the bottom and marketing intelligence is near the top.

Figure 10-4. This screenshot of Scout Labs' paid monitoring process shows what percentage of mentions of "Nike" come from Nike itself.

Paid Monitoring Tools

A number of paid options are available if your brand is large and gets lots of mentions. These tools can be helpful to identify positive and negative buzz, as well as to delegate responding duties within your company. Paid tools can make your life much easier if your brand is talked about frequently, as the free versions can get overwhelming and provide little organization.

Here are some of the more popular paid monitoring tools available today:

Radian6 (*http://www.radian6.com/cms/home/*)

> Radian6 is an enterprise-level social media monitoring system that monitors a variety of sources and features workflow functionality that allows you to delegate response tasks in your organization.

Scout Labs (*http://www.scoutlabs.com/*)

> Scout Labs is a less expensive alternative social media monitoring package. Starting at $99 per month, Scout Labs' charges are based on the number of terms you track, not the number of people at your company using it. Scout Labs also has integrated a number of natural language processing features to provide qualitative analysis alongside the more traditional quantitative data (see Figure 10-4).

Trackur (*http://www.trackur.com/*)

> Trackur is the least expensive of the three options mentioned here, and it offers many of the features of the others. Its pricing levels determine how often your searches are updated, from once every 12 hours to twice an hour.

Figure 10-5. *Domino's responded to the negative YouTube video on YouTube.*

Responding

Once you've identified a conversation about you or your brands, you must decide whether to engage and what to do when and if you decide to join in. Speed is vital, so start planning your response as soon as possible.

If a negative comment or conversation is something that your customer support team can handle, by all means, let them take care of it. If the problem is more of a public relations or brand crisis event, you need to decide whether your public response will draw more attention to the problem than it would have gotten naturally. Err on the side of responding, but at least ask yourself whether your response will draw unnecessary attention to the conversation.

Remain calm when a potential social media crisis begins to break out; follow the same protocol I talked about when responding to a negative comment on a review site. Becoming angry or defensive won't help your cause—it will only make matters worse. Do what you can to fix the problem that led to the gripe, and detail what you're going to do to make sure it doesn't happen again.

Responses to negative feedback should be communicated in the same medium in which the feedback was communicated; so, if someone posts an embarrassing video to YouTube—such as the video I mentioned in Chapter 1 showing the Domino's employees defiling food that was to be delivered to customers—your official apology should also be posted there (see Figure 10-5). If the original video was tweeted a lot, be sure to also spread your video on Twitter.

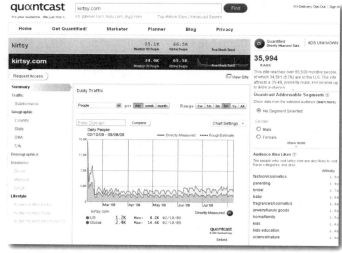

Figure 10-6. Quantcast's demographic information can help you get to know your audience.

Figure 10-7. Quantcast's content preference data indicates which category of sites Kirtsy users tend to frequent.

Research

Once you've started to monitor what is being said about you and your brand, you should get to know your audience. You want to know who they are, where they hang out online, and how they use the Web.

You're probably in your target market personally, and if not, you likely know a few people who are. Start with them (or yourself): ask them what their favorite sites are and what blogs they read. Build an initial list of these sites as starting points. Say you want to reach an older, more affluent female audience. Head on over to Quantcast and look at the data on sites from your initial list, such as Kirtsy, Sugarloving, BlogHer, and StumbleUpon. You'll see that of these sites, Kirtsy best matches your target audience (see Figure 10-6). Quantcast also gives you some great content preference data indicating which categories of sites Kirtsy users tend to frequent (see Figure 10-7):

- Fashion/Cosmetics
- Parenting
- Bridal
- Baby

- Fragrances/Cosmetics
- Jewelry/Luxury Goods
- Home/Family
- Kids

You'll notice that for some sites, Quantcast even offers links to other sites that share the same audience, which you can then use to further expand your seeding site list.

Another great place to find blogs about your topical niche is Alltop.com. This "virtual magazine rack" has over 700 categories of blogs covering nearly every subject.

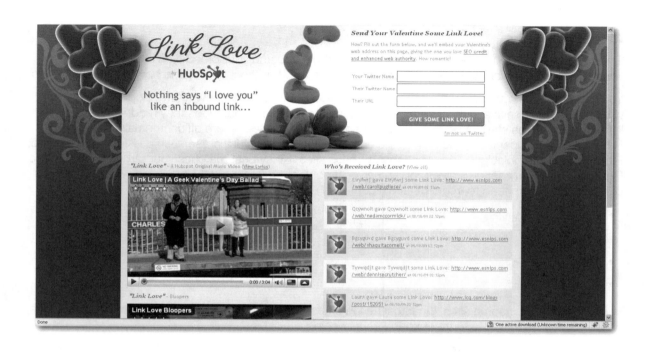

Figure 10-8. *Valentine's Day can be a great seasonal event on which to base a social media campaign.*

Campaigns Versus Ongoing Strategy

The actual work of social media marketing can be divided into two types: ongoing strategy and campaigns. Your *ongoing strategy* is the stuff you're doing on a regular basis: blogging, tweeting, contributing to forums, and so on. This is what you should be doing before your monitoring strategy finds an erupting crisis. Your ongoing work builds your brand and reputation.

When you've built a foundation of social media engagement with an established blog, Twitter account, and reputation on various social networks and sites, you can start launching *campaigns*. These should fit within your ongoing strategy and have specific goals and finite timelines. Viral videos, contests, and product launches should all be supported with dedicated campaigns. Seasonal and timely events are great things on which to base campaigns (see Figure 10-8).

Campaigns are the kinds of social media efforts that result in large but temporary spikes in traffic. I'll detail how to encourage those new users to become repeat visitors a little later in this chapter.

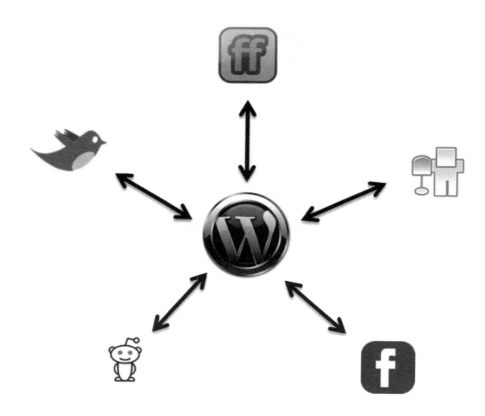

Figure 10-9. Your social media efforts should be integrated, and your blog should be the hub.

Integration

One of the central tenets of Web 2.0 is the idea that web applications should be able to share data and play nicely together. As Figure 10-9 shows, nearly every part of your social media marketing effort can integrate with at least one other part, and users of one kind of social media are likely to be users of other types; it makes sense to invite those who interact with you on Twitter to join your page on Facebook. Here are several examples:

- Your Facebook page can be connected to your Twitter account to pull in your tweets.
- Your LinkedIn account can include recent posts from your blog as well as presentations you've uploaded to SlideShare.
- Plug-ins can be used to automatically tweet your new blog posts.
- Your blog should have buttons for easy submission and voting on social news and bookmarking sites.
- Your YouTube videos can be embedded on your blog and on your Facebook page.
- You can link to your Second Life office from anywhere on the Web, including your blog, Facebook, and Twitter accounts.
- Your blog can automatically publish daily posts of the links you've bookmarked on Delicious.
- Your blog should have TweetMeme buttons to allow your readers to easily tweet about your content.

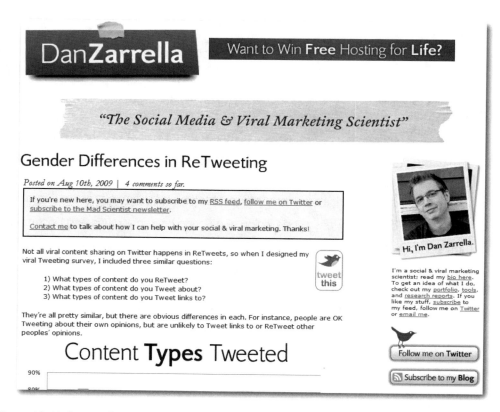

Figure 10-10. *In a sticky CTA, you can cross-promote to turn waves of traffic into return visitors.*

Calls to Action

A *call to action* (CTA) is an invitation you make to your website visitors to engage in some type of action that benefits your business aims—and hopefully theirs, too. CTAs usually have one of two goals: stickiness and conversion. *Sticky CTAs* turn ephemeral waves of traffic into return visitors, whereas *conversion-based CTAs* lead a visitor into your sales funnel. The former will be accepted by most communities, and the latter should be approached more delicately to avoid the appearance of hucksterism.

Sticky CTAs

Social media campaigns often bring visitors in spikes that quickly dissipate; a video goes viral, or a blog post hits Digg's front page, and you get thousands of visitors for a few days. You want these people to stick around, become engaged with your content, and help promote the next home run.

If your content is hosted on your blog—as much of it should be—you have an easy option: feed and email subscriptions. Consider including invitations in your content: "If you liked this post, subscribe to our blog for more." Another possibility is to offer exclusive content—an ebook, for instance—to subscribers only.

Social media sites with networking functionality also give you the option to encourage your readers to connect with you there. Ask your visitors to follow you on Twitter, fan your page on Facebook, or subscribe to your channel on YouTube. Don't forget to cross-promote; tweet a link to your YouTube channel, and ask people to subscribe (see Figure 10-10).

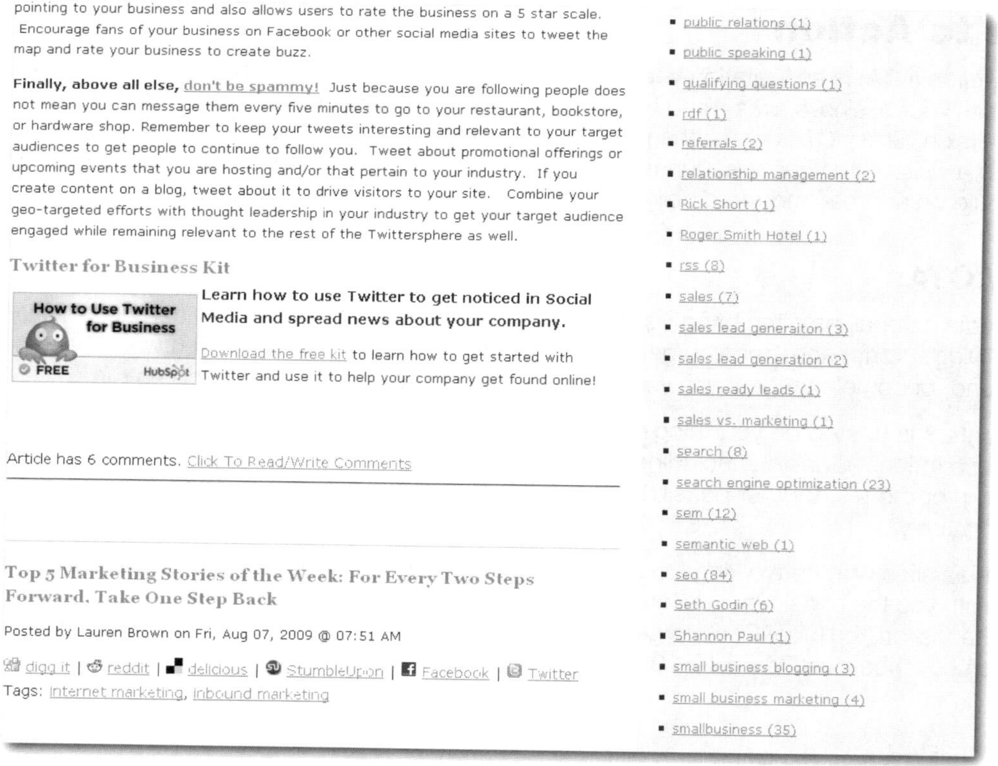

pointing to your business and also allows users to rate the business on a 5 star scale. Encourage fans of your business on Facebook or other social media sites to tweet the map and rate your business to create buzz.

Finally, above all else, don't be spammy! Just because you are following people does not mean you can message them every five minutes to go to your restaurant, bookstore, or hardware shop. Remember to keep your tweets interesting and relevant to your target audiences to get people to continue to follow you. Tweet about promotional offerings or upcoming events that you are hosting and/or that pertain to your industry. If you create content on a blog, tweet about it to drive visitors to your site. Combine your geo-targeted efforts with thought leadership in your industry to get your target audience engaged while remaining relevant to the rest of the Twittersphere as well.

Twitter for Business Kit

How to Use Twitter for Business

FREE HubSpot

Learn how to use Twitter to get noticed in Social Media and spread news about your company.

Download the free kit to learn how to get started with Twitter and use it to help your company get found online!

Article has 6 comments. Click To Read/Write Comments

Top 5 Marketing Stories of the Week: For Every Two Steps Forward, Take One Step Back

Posted by Lauren Brown on Fri, Aug 07, 2009 @ 07:51 AM

digg it | reddit | delicious | StumbleUpon | Facebook | Twitter

Tags: internet marketing, inbound marketing

- public relations (1)
- public speaking (1)
- qualifying questions (1)
- rdf (1)
- referrals (2)
- relationship management (2)
- Rick Short (1)
- Roger Smith Hotel (1)
- rss (8)
- sales (7)
- sales lead generaiton (3)
- sales lead generation (2)
- sales ready leads (1)
- sales vs. marketing (1)
- search (8)
- search engine optimization (23)
- sem (12)
- semantic web (1)
- seo (84)
- Seth Godin (6)
- Shannon Paul (1)
- small business blogging (3)
- small business marketing (4)
- smallbusiness (35)

Figure 10-11. A conversion-based call to action is designed to turn a visitor into a customer.

Conversion CTAs

Conversion-based CTAs are designed to turn a visitor into a customer (see Figure 10-11). There are two types of conversion-based CTAs, depending on your business model: leads and purchases. Very high-ticket items, such as cars or houses, as well as business-to-business transactions, start out as leads. A visitor becomes a lead when she fills out a form on your site that indicates that she's a potential customer. E-commerce sites, such as Amazon, don't have leads. Instead, visitors become customers by purchasing products directly.

Most lead-based businesses have (or should have) a simple conversion CTA in the form of a Contact Us page for interested parties to use. It is often more effective to ask a visitor to give you his information in return for some piece of content. You can require a reader to fill out a short form to download items such as ebooks and video webinars, and base your CTAs around these.

This type of CTA is more obviously commercial and should be used with more care than sticky CTAs. If someone has come to a blog post about a specific type of legal help, offer her an ebook about that area of the law, but don't shove it down her throat.

Takeaway Tips

- Remember your brand, but don't just use your old offline tricks in social media.

- Keep an eye on what people are saying about you, your products, and your competitors.

- Use your ongoing strategy to build a reputation, and then use short-term campaigns to kick-start specific offerings.

- Your social media marketing efforts should all work together.

- Use calls to action to entice your visitors to stick around and steer them to other offerings on your site.

- Don't forget the bottom line: be creative in how you convert social visitors to customers.

CHAPTER 11

Measurement

Introduction

To show business value and return on investment (ROI) for social media marketing campaigns, effective measurement is key. This chapter will focus on how you can prove the merit of the time and resources you invest in social media. It will help you convince your boss you're not just wasting time playing on Facebook.

In addition to conducting demographic research to identify which social sites your audience is using, you should also set goals with clearly defined levels for success. This chapter will discuss both of those topics, as well as teach you the basics of analytics on- and off-site.

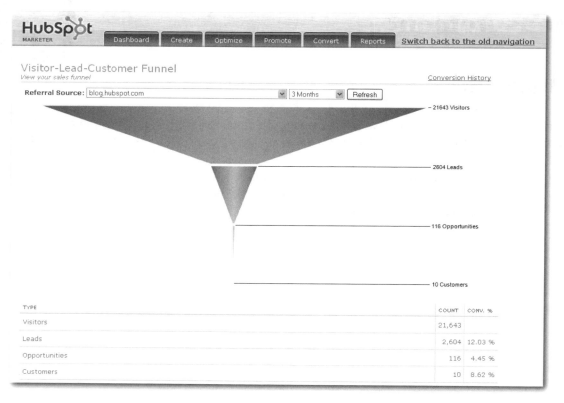

Figure 11-1. This is an example of closed-loop marketing analytics using HubSpot software.

Metrics

A *metric* is a standard unit of measurement; you measure how tall you are in the metric of inches or feet. I think about metrics for social media marketing in two categories: on-site and off-site. *On-site metrics* measure activity that takes place directly on your site, whereas *off-site metrics* measure activity that happens on other sites where you and your customers interact.

On-Site

This section will explore some of the basic on-site metrics you can use to measure your social media efforts.

ROI

The most important thing you can measure as a marketer is your return on investment, or how much money your efforts are contributing to your business. Is the cost of your investment in social media outweighed by the value it is providing?

All decent analytics packages allow you to track certain actions on your site, whether they are purchases or the completion of lead forms. By labeling visitors who've reached these goals, you'll be able to trace them back to their *referrers*, the sites that sent those visitors to you, and evaluate the effectiveness of each source.

If you're a lead-based company, estimate how much a lead is worth to you by calculating what percentage of leads turn into business and what your average customer is worth to you. Most software lets you configure their tracking mechanisms to include the actual price of a sale or this value per lead, so you can assign a monetary figure to each source of social media traffic. Some analytics systems allow integration with your sales systems to implement a concept called *closed loop marketing*. This means you can attribute closed business to specific leads, traffic sources, and campaigns (see Figure 11-1).

Figure 11-2. Google Analytics' engagement metrics indicate how engaged people are when they come to your site.

To calculate the actual ROI from your efforts, simply deduct the cost of your social media work (include monetary and time investments) from the income generated. If the result is a positive number, your investment has been profitable; if not, you should revisit your campaigns to see what is working and what is not. Also, pay attention to which sites and tactics are generating the most value. Not all businesses can beneficially engage all types of social media; focus on the ones that work for you.

Engagement

Not all of the people who come to your site from social media outlets are going to turn right into customers or leads, so you should also be measuring metrics that indicate how engaged people are when they come to your site. Most analytics software allows you to measure engagement metrics (see Figure 11-2).

The two easiest engagement metrics are time on-site and page views per visit. The longer a visitor spends on your site, or the more pages she reads, the deeper the relationship you're building with her. Hold on to sources of traffic that may not be generating direct sales (yet), but are generating highly engaged visitors, because as your traffic volumes increase, these sources are most likely to start producing conversions.

Bounce rates have been called the sexiest web metric. Analytical obsessions aside, they're a great way to identify which pages or sources of traffic are totally not working for you. A bounce is when I visit a page of your site and then don't go to any additional pages; I bounce right off your site. If you see a source of traffic that is generating a ton of bounces, first check which part of your site these people are landing on. Make sure that page is relevant to the reason they came to your site; if you had a tweet about cheap airline tickets, it shouldn't link to a page selling full-price first-class tickets. If they are landing on a reasonable page and still bouncing, that source of traffic might not be worth very much to you.

Figure 11-3. Subscriber metrics from FeedBurner provide information on the number of people consuming your feed and how they are consuming it.

But remember, an event such as going popular on Digg will generate a lot of bounces, but hopefully it will also generate some engaged visitors as well as links and subscribers, so balance bounce rates with the rest of your metrics.

If you have a blog—and you should have one—you can also measure the number of comments you're getting on each post. This is a good measure of the community you're building around your content. However, remember that a post without comments is not without value; controversial topics will generally get the most comments, but aren't necessarily doing the most good for your brand.

The other blog metric to keep a close eye on is your subscriber count. FeedBurner is a free product from Google that provides information on the number of people consuming your feed and how they are consuming it (see Figure 11-3). It also features an easy-to-set-up email subscription system that is a good way to deliver your content to nontechnical users. I've noticed that blog subscriptions are slow to rise, even long after a blog is getting tons of traffic, so don't expect overnight success here.

Eyeballs

Old-school marketers often come to the Web and start looking around for simple "eyeball" numbers (see Figure 11-4). They find hits, visits, and unique visitors. Of course, you should not ignore raw traffic counts, but be sure to look at them with a big grain of salt. The term *hits* typically means any request to a web server, and depending on the analytics system, that could include CSS files, images, and HTML, meaning that a single page view can have a dozen or more hits. Better than hits or even page views are the visitor and visit metrics.

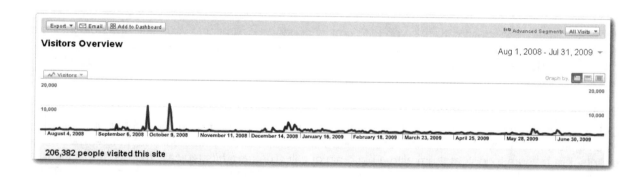

Figure 11-4. This is an example of pure eyeball-based metrics from Google Analytics.

Most software defines a single visit as one browser session with gaps between page requests no longer than 20 minutes. If I go to your site and poke around a little bit, read a few pages, and maybe fill out a form, that's one visit. If I come back tomorrow and do the same, I've added two visits to your reports. The visitor metric is an attempt to measure individual people coming to your site. If I don't delete my cookies and use the same computer both times, my two visits would be counted as one visitor.

As is possible with any kind of traffic on the Web, some types of social media successes will send a ton of people to your site who view one item and then leave. The majority of these visitors will not do very much for your business, but will create large spikes in the pure eyeball sections of your analytics reports—most real value on your site is created by people who push the needle in engagement metrics.

Off-Site

Because so many of your social media marketing activities occur in places other than your site, you should also be measuring a class of metrics that can be found off-site.

Twitter

On Twitter, the most obvious metric is the number of people following you. This represents your potential reach and is how most lists of top users are usually ranked. For marketing purposes, it is clearly better to have more followers, but it is not the only metric worth following. It is possible to get a ton of followers by simply following a ton of people and waiting for them to follow you back, but this does little to measure how engaged your followers are with your tweets.

Figure 11-5. Off-site Twitter analytics from TwitterCounter.com measure the number of people following you.

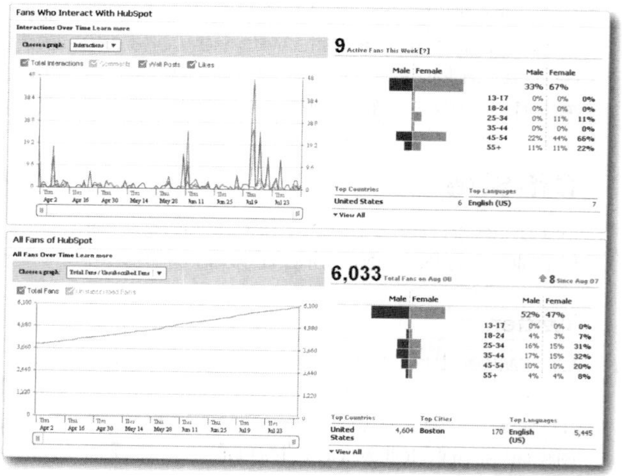

Figure 11-6. These Facebook page metrics indicate the gender and age of people who interact with HubSpot.

When people are actively following your micro conversations, they'll reply to you. This means that a count of how many times your username is mentioned in other people's tweets is a much better way to start understanding Twitter engagement. Figure 11-5 shows off-site Twitter analytics from TwitterCounter.com.

My favorite value—retweets—is harder to measure, but I believe it provides the best window into how influential you are on Twitter and what your total reach is. When I retweet someone else's content, I'm implicitly "voting" for his content as being valuable and worth sharing with my followers.

Facebook and LinkedIn

On Facebook and LinkedIn, your marketing efforts are focused on *pages* and *groups*, respectively, and although the words are different, they essentially mean the same thing.

The most basic metric to look at on both of these networks is the number of people who've joined your group or become fans of your page. LinkedIn does not provide any historical data like Facebook does, so you should record this number regularly by hand if you want to see how your group is growing.

Facebook also gives you more advanced data, but the "insights" platform is currently buggy and often does not actually return any information. The only statistic beyond the number of fans it does consistently provide is a demographic breakdown of the people interacting with your page, including gender and age. Although these numbers are interesting, they don't really provide that much actionable information. Figure 11-6 shows Facebook page metrics indicating the demographics of people who interact with HubSpot.

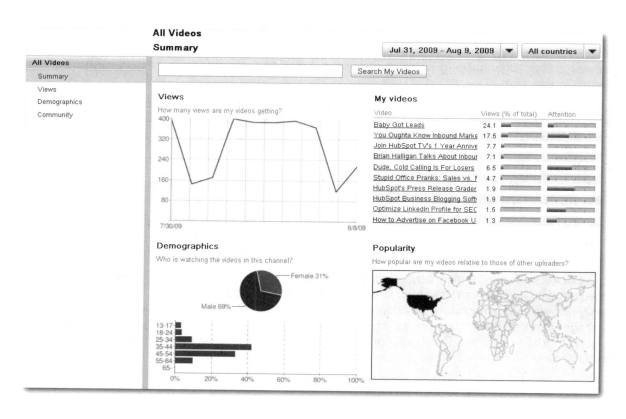

Figure 11-7. YouTube metrics show you which of your videos are getting the most views and who's viewing them.

Media-sharing sites

The most important metric for media-sharing sites is pretty straightforward: how many people viewed your image, presentation, or video. But since these are social media–sharing sites, you would be remiss to ignore how many people are commenting on your media. SlideShare and YouTube also allow viewers to stay connected to your content by following you on SlideShare and subscribing to your channel on YouTube. These last two numbers are similar to blog subscribers in that they will probably be the last to grow, but they are great indicators of a highly engaged audience (see Figure 11-7).

As I mentioned in other chapters, you should encourage your fans to upload media of their own to these sites, and when the media includes your product, brand, or you personally, you should tag it with your name. Simply doing a search for your name will then show you how many pieces of content other people have created about your company.

Social news and bookmarking sites

Since the point of marketing on social voting, news, and bookmarking sites is to get enough votes to become popular, you'll undoubtedly already be watching the key metric of votes. You can also monitor how many pieces of your content have been submitted to each site to understand whether your engagement with those communities is deeper (more votes on fewer pages) or wider (fewer votes on more pages).

Review sites

Clearly on a review site you should be looking at the number of reviews (more is better) and the quality of the reviews (higher-rated reviews are better). As I mentioned in Chapter 7, Yelp offers business owners great data about the amount of activity associated with their business listing. Traffic and search information is available, as is a simpler breakdown of the number and quality of reviews.

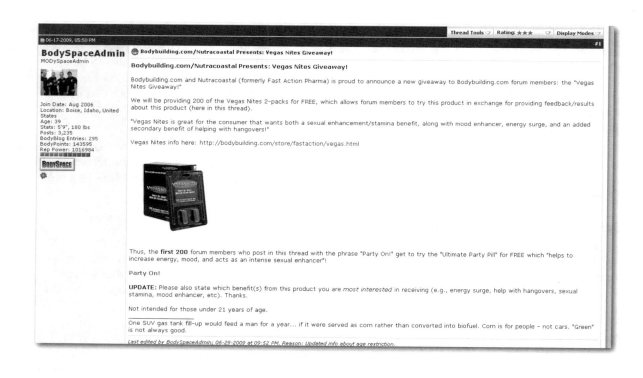

BodySpaceAdmin
MODySpaceAdmin

Join Date: Aug 2006
Location: Boise, Idaho, United States
Age: 39
Stats: 5'9", 180 lbs
Posts: 3,235
BodyBlog Entries: 295
BodyPoints: 143595
Rep Power: 1016984

Bodybuilding.com/Nutracoastal Presents: Vegas Nites Giveaway!

Bodybuilding.com/Nutracoastal Presents: Vegas Nites Giveaway!

Bodybuilding.com and Nutracoastal (formerly Fast Action Pharma) is proud to announce a new giveaway to Bodybuilding.com forum members: the "Vegas Nites Giveaway!"

We will be providing 200 of the Vegas Nites 2-packs for FREE, which allows forum members to try this product in exchange for providing feedback/results about this product (here in this thread).

"Vegas Nites is great for the consumer that wants both a sexual enhancement/stamina benefit, along with mood enhancer, energy surge, and an added secondary benefit of helping with hangovers!"

Vegas Nites info here: http://bodybuilding.com/store/fastaction/vegas.html

Thus, the **first 200** forum members who post in this thread with the phrase "Party On!" get to try the "Ultimate Party Pill" for FREE which "helps to increase energy, mood, and acts as an intense sexual enhancer"!

Party On!

UPDATE: Please also state which benefit(s) from this product you are *most interested* in receiving (e.g., energy surge, help with hangovers, sexual stamina, mood enhancer, etc). Thanks.

Not intended for those under 21 years of age.

_____

One SUV gas tank fill-up would feed a man for a year... if it were served as corn rather than converted into biofuel. Corn is for people - not cars. "Green" is not always good.

Last edited by BodySpaceAdmin; 06-29-2009 at 09:52 PM. Reason: Updated info about age restriction.

Figure 11-8. Post number and reputation metrics are available on many forums.

Forums

Forum marketing presents an interesting challenge for measurement. Obviously, if you're linking to your site—something you should do cautiously and only when it is very relevant to the discussion—you can track how many visitors you're sending and how valuable those people are to your business. But beyond that, the only other metrics you can measure in forums are posts and whatever reputation system may be available (see Figure 11-8). You should never post just to increase your numbers, but you should strive to regularly generate useful content, and eventually your post numbers will reflect how active you are. If the forums you're working in measure reputation or post quality by way of user ratings, pay close attention to how much other forum members like your posts.

Second Life

The only officially created metric available for measuring the success of a location in Second Life is traffic. It is based on a somewhat unknown algorithm that counts the number of people who pass through an area on a given day. If your location has a landmark-giving object, you can have it record the number of requests it receives, indicating how many people were engaged enough by your content to want an easy way to return to it. You can also easily record the number of unique visitors your location has, which may prove to be a more interesting figure than your traffic score. The same goes for recording requests received for other objects, such as the ones that hand out product information or your website URL. The user agent string in your web server log will also indicate whether a viewer came to you from the Second Life client browser. If you've created a group that you're using for marketing, you can also watch the number of members you have, but given the limitations of Second Life groups, this is probably a dubious strategy.

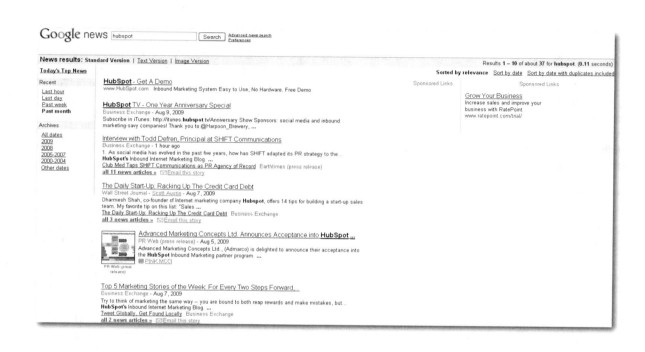

Figure 11-9. This Google News search shows earned media hits.

Earned media

The PR world gives us the concept of *earned media*, which is essentially the number of mentions your company gets in blogs, traditional news, and social media that it did not pay for. Successful social media efforts can generate a lot of buzz, so it is useful to track the number of times your company's name is mentioned on the Web. Easy ways to do this are with searches on Google News (see Figure 11-9) or simply Google Web.

Goal Setting

Before you start a new marketing initiative, you should set goals for your work. A simple example of this is to aim to generate a certain level of traffic, but as I mentioned before, pure eyeball metrics are problematic. The best goal you can set is for your social marketing efforts to lead to an amount of actual revenue for your business.

Your goals should include specific descriptions of success; don't have a goal of "increasing brand awareness." Rather, define exactly how you will measure awareness and an achievable threshold to shoot for. The actual metrics you'll use to measure your accomplishments toward a goal are called *key performance indicators* (KPIs). The various data points I detailed earlier can all be KPIs. For instance, if you're trying to increase your reach on Twitter, your KPI could be followers, and your stated goal should include an exact number of followers.

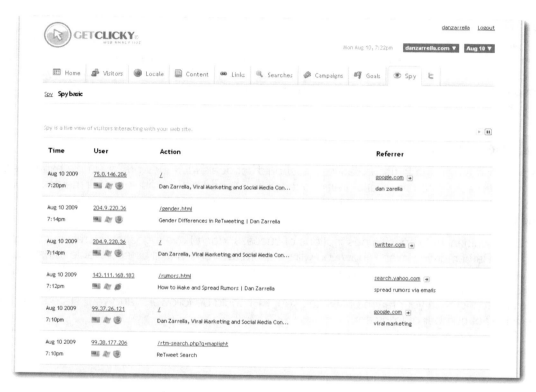

Figure 11-10. The paid version of Clicky offers a "spy" view, where you can watch activity on your site as it occurs.

Software

You can use a number of different software solutions to track your on-site metrics. Here are a few of the ones that are the most popular and easiest to use, but be aware that there are many more than I've listed here:

Google Analytics (*http://www.google.com/analytics/*)

> One of the most popular analytics systems, Google Analytics is a free and robust package from Google. It allows you to track eyeball and engagement metrics, as well as goals, including direct purchases and leads. There is a delay between when a user performs an action on your site and when your reports will reflect the action, but for most companies, Google Analytics provides plenty of data.

Clicky (*http://getclicky.com/*)

> One of my favorite analytics packages, Clicky has free and paid versions of its software. The statistics are real-time, meaning there is no delay as with Google Analytics, and the paid version offers a "spy" view, where you can watch activity on your site happen in real time (see Figure 11-10). This is especially useful for social news and bookmarking marketing efforts because you can see when a new site starts sending traffic to you and add buttons to your content for that site.

HubSpot (*http://www.hubspot.com/*)

> The company I work for, HubSpot, offers analytics as a part of its inbound marketing software. It is different from the data offered by Google Analytics in that it is designed for marketing professionals, includes lead information, and integrates with Salesforce.com to allow for closed-loop marketing measurement.

Takeaway Tips

- Measure ROI as best you can; actual sales amounts or closed leads are best.

- Focus on engagement metrics over pure eyeball metrics.

- Don't forget to measure your performance on external social sites.

- Set achievable goals, and know how you're going to measure your progress.

- Select an easy-to-use web analytics package.

Acknowledgments

This book would not have been possible without the help of a lot of people, and I'm sure I'm going to forget some names.

First, I would like to thank Pete Cashmore, Brett Tabke, Luther Lowe, Tara Kirchner, and Jennifer Zeszut for their valuable insights and inside looks into their businesses. Sharing the experiences, opinions, challenges, and successes they have encountered over the years provided me with a unique perspective on how social media can, and should, be used—as well as how it shouldn't.

Thanks also to Laurel Ruma (@laurelatoreilly), Rick Burnes (@rickburnes), Alison Driscoll (@alisond), Matt Robinson (@mrobins), Samantha Strauss (@sfsam22), JD Lasica (@jdlasica), Tristan Walker (@tristanwalker), and Jordyne Wu (@jordyne) for their obsessive yet ultimately helpful edits, suggestions, criticisms, and comments. Everyone needs an editor, and I was lucky enough to have so many who excel in their specialties and never scrimp on feedback.

Last but not least, thanks to @bwhalley, @ellieeille, @mvolpe, @kylepaice, @dharmesh, @abdinoor, @karenrubin, @bsimi, @tedChris, @ed, @guykawasaki, @briansolis, @GabVaz, @eddiehebert, @webaddict, @yourfriendEVAN, @TheRealBenSmith, @YoavShapira, @SharonFeder, @adamhirsch, @tamar, @msaleem, @joselinmane, @repcor, and countless others who have helped me in one way or another. Every interaction went into this book, in some way.

And of course, thank you to my mother, sister, girlfriend, and BJ for putting up with me all these years.

Index

Colophon

The cover, heading, and text font is Helvetica Neue.

About the Author

Dan Zarrella has written extensively about the science of viral marketing, memetics, and social media on his own blog and for a variety of popular industry blogs, including Mashable, CopyBlogger, ReadWriteWeb, Plagiarism Today, ProBlogger, Social Desire, CenterNetworks, Nowsourcing, and SEOScoop.

He has been featured in *The Twitter Book* (O'Reilly), the *Financial Times*, the *New York Post*, the *Boston Globe*, *Forbes*, *Wired*, the *Wall Street Journal*, Mashable, and TechCrunch. He was recently awarded Shorty and Semmy awards for social media and viral marketing.

Dan has spoken at PubCon, Search Engine Strategies, Convergence '09, 140: The Twitter Conference, WordCamp Mid Atlantic, Social Media Camp, Inbound Marketing Bootcamp, and the Texas Domains and Developers Conference. He currently works as an inbound marketing manager at HubSpot.

Try the online edition free for 45 days

Get the information you need when you need it, with Safari Books Online. Safari Books Online contains the complete version of the print book in your hands plus thousands of titles from the best technical publishers, with sample code ready to cut and paste into your applications.

Safari is designed for people in a hurry to get the answers they need so they can get the job done.

You can find what you need in the morning, and put it to work in the afternoon. As simple as cut, paste, and program.

To try out Safari and the online edition of the above title FREE for 45 days, go to www.oreilly. com/go/safarienabled and enter the coupon code XAYOHAA.

To see the complete Safari Library visit: safari.oreilly.com